GURGAON DIARIES

Debeshi Gooptu is a business journalist turned digital content strategist and entrepreneur. With more than twenty years of experience in print and television (*Business Standard, Business Today, Plus Channel*) and higher education (British Council, Canadian High Commission, Intel Asia Electronics), she runs an online research consultancy for overseas education organization and works as a digital content strategy head for Digiqom, a digital media agency. Debeshi is also the India editor for Innovation Enterprise, a Singapore-headquartered publication tracking trends in technology and innovation in Asia-Pacific. She frequently blogs for Huffington Post and runs 'The Gurgaon Diaries', a successful blog. In 2015, she self-published an e-book (with the same name) comprising few of her stories from the blog on Amazon Kindle Select. The book has done extremely well with readers across the world requesting for more writing in this genre.

GURGAON DIARIES

Life, Work and Play in Drona's Village

Debeshi Gooptu

RUPA

Published by
Rupa Publications India Pvt. Ltd 2017
7/16, Ansari Road, Daryaganj
New Delhi 110002

Sales centres:
Allahabad Bengaluru Chennai
Hyderabad Jaipur Kathmandu
Kolkata Mumbai

Copyright © Debeshi Gooptu, 2018

This is a work of fiction. Names, characters, places and incidents are either the product of the author's imagination or are used fictitiously and any resemblance to any actual person, living or dead, events or locales is entirely coincidental.

All rights reserved.
No part of this publication may be reproduced, transmitted,
or stored in a retrieval system, in any form or by any means,
electronic, mechanical, photocopying, recording or otherwise,
without the prior permission of the publisher.

ISBN: 978-81-291-XXXX-X

First impression 2018

10 9 8 7 6 5 4 3 2 1

The moral right of the author has been asserted.

Printed by

This book is sold subject to the condition that it shall not, by way
of trade or otherwise, be lent, resold, hired out, or otherwise circulated,
without the publisher's prior consent, in any form of binding
or cover other than that in which it is published.

*For Baba, who taught me how to tell stories
and find humour in impossible situations.
For Gurgaon, a city I've grown to love
more than my birthplace, Kolkata.*

Contents

Introduction   *xi*

Life

1. Don't Stand So Close to Me — 3
2. On a Sausage and a Prayer — 7
3. Fishy Business — 11
4. Naseeruddin — 15
5. It's Not Halloween Yet but the Monsters Are Already Out — 19
6. Sadly Bengali — 23
7. Sadly Bengali Again — 27
8. Gangnam Style — 31
9. Modesty Is Back — 35
10. A Sin to Tan? — 38
11. Nip Tuck and a Shot in the Butt — 41
12. The Other Monkey in My Life — 45
13. Neither Shaken nor Stirred — 49
14. Holy Cow — 53
15. Brawn and the Beautiful — 57
16. Fifty Shades of Grey — 61
17. Things That Go Bump in the Night — 64
18. Lost in Translation — 68
19. Time to Change — 71
20. Kids off the Menu — 75

21.	Fat and Loving It	78
22.	The Ghost in the Machine	81
23.	Pesky Pigeons	83
24.	Sweet Memories	86
25.	Freedom Calling	89
26.	Irritable Bowel Syndrome	92
27.	Hellish Symphony	95
28.	Nightmare on Selfie Street	98
29.	Turning Japanese	101
30.	It's a Dog's Life	104
31.	Outside the Box	108
32.	Driving Miss Daisy	111
33.	Buzz	114
34.	Beauty and the Beastly	117
35.	Santa Claus Is Coming to Town	120
36.	Mind Your Language	124
37.	Sex and the City	128
38.	Doctor Doctor	132
39.	The Ladies of Gurugram	135
40.	What's in a Name?	138

Work

1.	Mrs Invisible	145
2.	Waterlogged	148
3.	Friday Dressing	152
4.	Drive to Hell	156
5.	All the Village Is an App	159
6.	I Hunger for You	163
7.	Parking Games	166

Play

1. Doing Coffee — 171
2. Run for Your Life — 175
3. Twang, Bang, Thank You Ma'am — 179
4. Chicken Is the New Black — 183
5. To Smear or Not to Smear — 187
6. Adventures of the Road Runner — 191
7. The Horrors of Halloween — 195
8. Ek Bottle Vodka — 199
9. Party Pooper — 202
10. Gurgaon Ink — 207
11. Unfaithfully Yours — 211
12. Gurugram Gymming — 216
13. Every Dog Has its Day — 219
14. Between a Rock and a Hard Place — 223

Introduction

Pick up any Indian history book, epic like the *Mahabharata* or you could just Google search, if you're so inclined, and you will discover that Gurgaon or Gurugram (as it's been renamed recently) was gifted to Guru Dronacharya by the Pandavas and Kauravas in return for training in military arts. While the legends of the mythical village are woven around the warrior mystic who trained the protagonists of the Indian epic, the Millennium City or India's Singapore, as it is popularly called, owes its rapid growth to globalization and the BPO boom. Some say Gurgaon got its name from the jaggery (gur) that was sold in markets in and around this region. While I have no idea about the authenticity of these stories, one thing is for certain. There is nothing remotely rustic about the concrete jungle that is modern-day Gurgaon. Other than the cows!

The Millennium City is a paradox. The swanky malls and skyscrapers with their glass and steel facades playing host to some of the world's largest conglomerates and brands coexist with pothole-ridden roads where shiny new Mercs and Lamborghinis vie for space with autos and cycle rickshaws. There are designer stores, emporiums, Starbucks coffee franchises, international restaurant chains and across the road are food trucks, roadside vans peddling chole bhatures and dhabas selling tandoori chicken and bread pakodas.

Gurugram's one-million denizens are a motley crew. There are aunties, mashimas, Jat boys and girls, corporate executives, call centre workers, businessmen, real estate dealers, fitness enthusiasts, socialites, maids, ragpickers, rickshaw pullers and garbage collectors—a melting pot of people from all around the world. All of them contribute towards creating Gurgaon's rather unique community whose sense of style, etiquette and language has no parallel.

The story of how modern-day Gurgaon came into being is quite remarkable. How a quiet hamlet in Haryana transformed into a leading IT services and industrial hub with the third highest per capita income in India is the stuff of legends. It is as remarkable as the thought that the Kauravas once ran amok in the brilliant yellow mustard fields that line National Highway 8, which connects Gurgaon to Delhi and the rest of the world. I can almost hear Guru Dronacharya screaming at the top of his lungs, ordering them to focus on their lessons!

Nineteen years ago, when I first moved here from Kolkata, all that Gurgaon had were empty spaces. I still remember the fleeting glimpse of the village from an airplane window—wide, open, empty spaces with or without greens. A bumpy touchdown later, I discovered that the village had life. There were a handful of multinational corporations and call centres, Genpact and Maruti being the star attractions. There were condominiums, independent kothis and a few grocery shops, tailoring boutiques and hole-in-the-wall eateries selling rajma chawal, tandoori chicken and jeera aloo. The eatery owners actually heaved a sigh of relief every time you told them you wanted the food packed to take home. That meant they wouldn't have to worry about finding you a place to sit! There were no fancy malls, restaurants, lounges or pubs to hang out in. It was North India's quiet little Gaulish village before the fish started flying around. In Gurgaon's case, it was dog poop!

Over the years, I witnessed globalization and rapid economic growth transform the sleepy Haryanvi hamlet into a throbbing, bustling urban hub. The empty spaces got filled up by skyscrapers, the grocery stores turned into supermarkets and the local boutiques run by Punjabi aunties morphed into swanky malls and designer stores. Rajma chawal and jeera aloo became passé. Sushi, bulgogi and imported truffles were de rigueur. There was an influx of migrants from all around the world and greasy real estate agents were suddenly knocking at your door. Gurgaon was a success story everyone wanted a piece of.

The contrasts and contradictions of this rags-to-riches story were too apparent to ignore. They were both hilarious and poignant, ironic and bittersweet at the same time. With the glitzy hub having come up in no time, it didn't have the infrastructure to support the demands of burgeoning development. There weren't proper roads, lighting or sanitation—the three requisites of any city that aspires to be modern. Realization began to set in. Despite the outward, fancy trappings, Gurgaon was still a village.

Come monsoon season each year and all hell would break loose. The roads would be submerged leaving residents and office-goers stranded inside their fancy condominiums. Water would creep into homes and elevators. There would be mayhem on the streets with the traffic snarls and tempers rising. Winter season brought with it the problem of heavy fog and inadequate street lighting. Add to that the incessant power outages. Every season brought with it a checklist of problems.

Gurgaon's success story was developing holes almost as deep as the ones on its roads. The earthquakes only made it worse. Gurgaon was high-risk seismic zone IV. The roads were ridden with gigantic craters leading to some really unnavigable terrain. Driving through the city was like dirt-track racing on most days. There were no pavements either. So a walk was completely out of the question, unless you were in a mood to die!

The BPO boom also had an unlikely beneficiary. The language of the rustic hamlet had changed in a manner that would have put Otto Jespersen out of business had the Danish linguist been alive. People were now conversing in a language that can, at best, be described as a fusion of Haryanvi, Hindi and English, peppered liberally with Americanisms.

There were other, subtle changes in the colour of the place that were hard to spot at first. While, on the one hand, wallets were getting deeper due to the industrial and property boom, there were people living in abject poverty. There were more and more beggars on the streets and police stations were recording an increase in crime. Petty theft and chain-snatching had now progressed to murders and rapes. Gurgaon was bursting at the seams. The construction boom had also made the air in the city unsafe to breathe. Air quality index in Gurgaon had touched the 356-mark making it the most polluted city in India.

That's when the government decided that it was time for a name change to celebrate the historical heritage of the city. The Dronacharya connection had to be revived. Gurgaon was renamed Gurugram. The Millennium City officially turned back into a village and what a journey it has been!

These are my stories of the two-decade-long journey. The journey from Gurgaon to Gurugram. Or was it the other way around? There have been so many changes over the years that confusion is inevitable. Even the blue cows that once roamed about near the Aravalli Hills have now turned white. Turn the pages and find out what it means to live, work and play in Gurugram, warrior Drona's village. Whether you are here to stay or are just passing through, there's enough wisdom in here to rival the ancient Guru's knowledge!

Life

*All is Fair in Love and War.
In this Village at least!*

1.

Don't Stand So Close to Me

At a party last weekend, I overheard a friend regaling another with an amusing anecdote about an elderly colleague who had tried to make a play for her at a book launch recently. Rolling her eyes in mock exasperation, she went on to describe how the man, a beady-eyed gentleman in his late 50s, had stood very close to her as he tried to chat her up. 'He was barely giving me room to breathe, he was that close!' she exclaimed indignantly. The other woman's 'Ugh, how creepy,' was the last thing I heard as I moved away with my glass of wine, way past earshot.

Gazing at the vast Gurgaon skyline, dotted with tall buildings, twinkling with lights, I pondered on whether the man in question could be held guilty for a fault most of us Indians have. Oh, don't get me wrong. I'm not talking about the lechery bit. Though, seeing the way this country is headed, it seems many of us have that defect as well. What I am talking about is a complete lack of awareness about the concept of personal space.

A few weeks back, while I was at the checkout counter of an upscale clothing store at a mall in Gurgaon, I felt something sharp nudging me in the small of my back. Looking back angrily, ready with a string of abuses to hurl out, I found a short, rotund lady standing so close to me that the credit card she was brandishing was jabbing me in the small of my back. I gave her a dirty look and moved up as close as I could to the counter, away from her. She did the same, and now she was even closer. I could smell the garlic pickle she had consumed with her paranthas for lunch. There was nothing more I could do. I couldn't climb over to the other side, on top of the salesman's lap, could I? Helpless, I held my breath, waiting for my card to be swiped, collected my bags and ran.

It happened again recently. After finishing a round of hectic grocery shopping at the neighbourhood store, I had reached the checkout counter to find that it was empty. I placed my basket on top of the counter and the young shop boy instantly tipped the contents of the basket and got busy creating a bill on his computer for everything I had bought. Suddenly, like a bat out of hell, a young woman came charging towards us. She gave me a slight push with her elbow and banged her shopping basket down on the counter, roughly moving mine out of the way. There was hardly enough space for one basket, leave alone two. A few things, such as carton of milk and a loaf of bread from my basket nearly fell on the floor. I caught them just in time with my hands. The man behind the counter stared at her aghast. I turned around to look at her coldly.

'Excuse me,' I said. 'I'm still not finished paying my bill. Can you move yourself *and* your basket slightly so that this gentleman can complete my transaction.' I pointed towards the checkout clerk who was still gaping at her.

'No, my basket is very heavy. I can't move it,' she mumbled rudely, looking away.

'I'm sure it's heavy but you don't need to pile it on top of mine. If it's heavy, please put it down on the floor. When I'm finished, you can get started.'

As I said that, I pushed her basket roughly away from mine.

It would have fallen on the floor had she not caught it quickly. Something in my tone told her not to answer back. Instead, she moved back a few steps, placing the basket down on the floor. I could see the checkout guy suppress a smile as he went back to scanning price tags for the bill. Soon I was finished paying for my stuff. Before I turned to leave, I looked back to where the woman was standing, mouthed a soundless thank you and walked out of the store.

How many times has this happened to you? At a mall, while paying your bills or even while having a conversation—the person in front (or back) standing too close. It happens to me all the time. I'm perpetually troubled by people who stand too close to me at queues, subjected to well-meaning or rude jabs of plastic baskets or whatever they are carrying.

I think it's great that some Gurgaon retail stores have made it mandatory for customers to wait at a certain spot till the checkout counter is free. No crowding behind the person who is paying for the things bought at the counter. No more basket warfare or unintended pokes. The situation at the outback queue is a different matter altogether. There's a commotion out there too. Banks and airport immigration counters have this system as well. It's kind of a double-edged sword. But at least there aren't people annoying you when you are paying the bills.

I remember advising all my students, when working as a counsellor with the British Council and the Canadian Embassy, to respect other people's personal space when they travelled to universities abroad. 'Maintain some distance when you are talking to people, they don't like people getting too close,' I would say to the eager youngsters, holding my arm out and gingerly stepping back all the while as I spoke so that I could maintain that safe distance myself.

Never worked!

Don't Stand So Close to Me

I think a study of Proxemics should be included in the school curriculum so that students are aware of the concept of personal space from early on in their lives.

I can't help but grin when I think about that fat lady who had poked me with her credit card. She needed a course in Proxemics too. On a bad day, I might have whacked her really hard with my handbag. She didn't deserve that. She certainly wasn't making a pass at me. She just didn't know any better. Most of us don't. As for the elderly Casanova who was trying to romance my friend, he doesn't know better either. But, a few thwacks of a leather handbag may just do the trick for him!

2.

On a Sausage and a Prayer

It is said that the sins of the past catch up with you eventually. I didn't think it would happen quite so soon with me. Or that retribution would arrive in the form of an angry, tearful ten-year-old demanding answers.

'Why don't you fast for Navratri?' she hurled at me, in between sobs, tears streaming down her face. She had just returned from school, rucksack still on her shoulder, hair all dishevelled. I stared at her for a moment, wondering whether I had heard her right. And then it came again, the question. Only this time, she had stopped crying and was glowering at me, waiting for my reply.

Navratri is a festival which involves the worship of Goddess Durga, coinciding with the Bengali Durga Puja. In North India, during the navratri, people fast over a period of seven days, breaking the fast with the traditional meal of pooris, chana and sweet halwa. For us Bengalis, on the other hand, it is a period of feasting and festivity. Puja, for us, indicates a period of excessive gluttony and gastronomy.

'We don't follow Navratri sweetheart. That is a North Indian festival, we are from…' I began hesitantly, getting ready to offer the little girl a lesson in the cultural differences between the Eastern and Northern parts of the country.

'But I've never seen you fast for any puja, Ma,' she shot back at me. She was persistent, I'll give her that. Not to mention an eidetic memory. She had my genes after all.

The time had come. I had to confess, right here and now.

All my life I have shied away from ritual worship. This is something that has gotten me into immense trouble, especially after I got married, with my extended family being overtly religious. Now, before you label me as an atheist, let me point out that I've always believed in God but I have never felt the need to have a special time or a special way to show my love or appreciation for the Almighty.

So while others of my faith thronged to the temples or the pandals during festivals such as Durga Puja, I stayed away. Religion to me was a personal affair, not meant to be shared with the community at large. It didn't involve any form of display or ostentation. I talked to God all the time, well, most of the time anyway. I liked to call it my 24-hour hotline with God.

As far as fasting was concerned, that had always been completely out of the question. I can't torture myself or abuse my body to prove a point or score brownie points with the Almighty. I don't believe God is judging us anyway. To each his own. Or so I've always believed.

But, as I stared at the little face in front of me, a face I loved more than life itself, all swollen and teary-eyed, I could sense that things may have to change pretty soon.

'I don't believe in fasting,' I volunteered weakly, wondering what it was that had worked my daughter up so much.

It turned out that she had been teased by a bunch of her classmates at lunchtime. Just when she was getting ready to bite into the sausage bun I had given her for tiffin, the rest of the girls had gathered around her. If I hadn't known any better, I might have referred to them as the mini hindutva brigade! The little girls were aghast that a Hindu girl, one of their own, was tucking into non-vegetarian fare during Navratri when their own mothers were fasting and eating precious little. Her feeble 'we don't follow this festival' had not worked.

They had lectured her, on and on, till in the end my daughter had put away the bun and decided to eat it on her way back home, in the safety of the school bus.

'I don't want to eat any non-vegetarian food for tiffin as long as this Navratri is on,' my daughter insisted sullenly. 'Those girls will pounce on me again if I do.'

I couldn't help but wonder whether this is what that poor Muslim man felt, just hours before his death, when he saw the angry mob gather outside his door accusing him of having eaten beef. That was in a village in Uttar Pradesh where the villagers were mostly illiterate and provoked by vested interests into taking the extreme step.

I couldn't believe that little girls belonging to modern, literate, well-to-do families, studying in top schools could be indoctrinated in this manner. What belief system were these girls going to grow up with? That it was acceptable to be intolerant? That bullying anyone who didn't conform to their scheme of things was okay?

I could feel my blood pressure rising, my heart beating a little faster, my face feeling warm. 'Don't be silly,' I reprimanded, trying to sound forceful, not feeling anything close to fortitude in reality. 'Like I said, it's not our festival. We celebrate Durga Puja in a completely different way. Haven't you seen that? Have you seen anyone fasting during our Puja? Everyone is busy eating fish fries and cutlets. You don't need to pay attention to what the other girls say.'

She was staring at the floor, eyes fixed to a spot near her shoes, dirt tracks on her cheeks from the tears. I saw her mouth twist into a little smile. Possibly at the thought of those delectable fish

On a Sausage and a Prayer 9

cutlets. My heart melted. She was my daughter, an incorrigible foodie like me!

I fired my last salvo, 'Do they follow our festivals?' No reply. I realized that it was futile. The ten-year old was resolute, standing her ground, even refusing my offer to write a note to her class teacher.

I knew that I would have to fall in line, and fast. The stomach growled in revolt. The heart sank. The sausage buns in the fridge that I had bought from the bakery next door would have to wait for another few days.

I had to be devout and fast. I hope you are happy, God!

3.
Fishy Business

I stood in front of the tray at the fishmongers' contemplating the rows of dead fish that lay on their bed of ice. There was a signboard on top that had their names neatly printed on it—Carp, Katla, Pomfret, Bekti, Red Snapper, Prawns. All I saw were glazed, lifeless eyes staring back at me, glistening bodies all in a row. I shivered and gingerly touched the scales of the one nearest to me—it felt cold and clammy. I flinched and moved my hand away. Looking around, I spotted a young boy hovering nearby. I yelled out in Hindi, 'Are these fresh?' The boy stared blankly at me, shrugged and moved away.

I sighed. Buying fish is an ordeal for me. Unlike most Bengalis, I'm not terribly fond of eating fish and find no pleasure in shopping for cold, dead things that I have to poke and prod in order to guess how fresh they are or how long ago they died. I find the whole process slightly revolting. Add to that the pain of communicating in Hindi with local Haryanvi fishmongers trying hard to explain what I want and how I want it cut.

My friends tell me that I should drive down to Chittaranjan Park in Delhi and shop at the markets there. Chittaranjan Park is a mini-Kolkata, the largest settlement of Bengalis in Delhi NCR. There are several markets selling a mind-boggling variety of goods—from aam shotto (a sweet and tart leathery mango delicacy) to sandesh (a Bengali sweet). The shopkeepers all speak Bengali and you can haggle with them and get the freshest and choicest cuts of meat, fish and vegetables.

Drive for several hours to buy fish? Nah, I don't have that kind of commitment. I would rather struggle at the stores here. So you will find me yelling at the top of my voice instead: *'Nahi! steak pieces nahi.'*

Who on earth gets fish cut into steak pieces for a good old-fashioned Bengali curry with potatoes and cauliflower. *'Mujhe chhota, round round chahiye.'* I find myself struggling to describe the traditional Bengali cuts of fish which involve leaving the head and the tail portion of the fish intact. *'Tail or head cut nahi chahiye, usko rehne dijiye,'* I say in frustration, finally resorting to gesturing with my hands and fingers, providing serious entertainment for the fishmongers and fellow shoppers.

Most of the young chaps who slice the fish into pieces for the customers aren't really fishmongers. They are just extra hands hired by the store management without any idea of how meat or fish should be cut. They stare at me curiously when I babble on about how I want the fish to be cut. 'This one is mad,' their look suggests. 'There she goes again!'

I remember accompanying my favourite aunt to buy fish when I was a little girl growing up in Kolkata. Looking back, I recall the busy market, thronging with people and the whiff of fresh vegetables and fish in the air; makeshift stalls alongside dingy alleys lit by solitary bulbs here and there with a narrow lane running in between; heaps of fresh vegetables and fruit piled on the raised platforms where the hawkers sat; and above all, the excitement. The fish sellers would be in a separate part of the market. The alleys became slimier in this part and one had to watch one's step. The smells were different too—stronger, more pungent. Different kinds of fish would be heaped over the slabs. The ones alive would be swimming around merrily in gigantic metal bowls. No icy morgues existed in those days. Bengali film music would be blaring from the small transistors placed alongside a few of the stalls; perhaps to drive away the monotony.

I remember the easy camaraderie between my aunt and her fish seller. I remember his name was Kartik. They exchanged smiles and conspiratorial whispers when others were around. He would always make sure she got the best and the freshest of the lot before others could take their pick. It was a special kind of connect. I remember the smile on her face as she walked out of the market, carrying heavy bags laden with fish and vegetables, me in tow, a skip in her step, cheeks flushed as though she was a woman in love.

'Sounds like your aunt had an affair with the fishmonger yaar,' one of my friends joked. 'What's so special about buying fish? You just go to the shop, tell the chap at the counter what you want and they give it to you. The way you talk about it, it's as though they had something else going on, other than fish,' she guffawed.

'You wouldn't understand it,' I said irritably. The truth is she wouldn't. For years, I've puzzled over the rapport my aunt and the fishmonger seemed to share—that special connection. In the cold, rather mechanical world of grocery stores that I'm familiar with, I've never shared a human connection with anyone. Just routine picking out stuff off shelves and lugging it to the counter where unsmiling people just dump it in cloth bags and hand me the bill. Never a smile or a word exchanged. I couldn't blame my friend for thinking there was hanky-panky afoot.

'Didi,' I hear a brusk voice behind me, breaking my reverie abruptly. I turn around to see a tall, slightly overweight youth staring at me curiously. He's wearing a shabby AC/DC t-shirt and a pair of baggy denims. 'You asked about the fish?' he said haltingly, in Hindi. 'We got it this morning. It's very fresh.'

I've never been addressed as 'Didi' outside of Kolkata. Here, it's always 'Madamji' or 'Memsahib.'

I pointed to the one I had touched earlier, 'Can you cut this for me into medium pieces?' I asked, avoiding the word steak.

'*Steak piss chahiye ya gada peti?*' he asked, slightly hesitantly.

'Are you a Bengali?' I was quite sure what his answer would be. Those familiar Bengali words 'gada peti' indicating Bengali-style cuts of fish were a dead giveaway.

The face broke into a big grin and a violent nod. And in that instant, my whole world transformed. I could almost hear the birds sing. That's when it hit me. A relationship between a Bengali woman and her fishmonger is special. A once-in-a-lifetime connect, not just fishy business! I'm sure many would agree with me on this.

I've been buying fish every week since then!

4.

Naseeruddin

Every year, around this time, Naseeruddin goes home for a month.

Naseeruddin is a small, thin man with skin the colour of burnt earth. He's not someone you would ordinarily notice. Or even spare a moment thinking about, leave alone write about. I wouldn't either. But he's a Very Important Person in my scheme of things and it's only fair that I dedicate a few lines to tell his story.

Naseeruddin is my chauffeur. It's a job he's taken up voluntarily. I haven't officially hired him. I don't really need a chauffeur. Most of the places I frequent such as the grocery store or my daughter's school or even the neighbourhood shopping mall (if I'm feeling particularly adventurous) are within walking distance of my home. I don't need transport to get there.

But there's no getting away from Naseeruddin! He's always waiting near the gate with his trademark toothy grin, ready to whisk me away, brushing aside my feeble protests. These days, I don't even bother. As soon as I spot him, I walk across meekly to him. I climb onto the rickshaw carefully avoiding the torn leather that rises in the middle of the seat like the folds of a flower in bloom. Shreds of gaily-coloured plastic, remnants of what was once a cover, hang loosely from the metal hood of the rickshaw.

One 'tring' of his rickshaw horn and we are off.

Naseeruddin is very different from others of his ilk. He doesn't have an attitude, never grumbles or misses a day of work, except for his customary month-long leave once a year. But then, one can't really compare him to other chauffeurs for he doesn't drive a swanky Mercedes, Audi or Toyota. He owns a rickety cycle rickshaw, purchased for a 'princely' sum of five thousand rupees.

'Where are you from, Naseeruddin?' I asked him one evening as we returned from my daughter's piano lesson. I was hugging the six-year-old close to me so that she didn't fall off the speeding rickshaw. Her chubby hands tried to grab the plastic hanging from the hood of the rickshaw from within the confines of my arms, giggling all the while as she missed.

'Uttar Dinajpur, Didi,' he replied cheerfully. Uttar Dinajpur is a district in the northern part of West Bengal. It is one of the most backward districts in the country with a sizeable Muslim population. 'Many rickshaw pullers in Gurgaon come from there. I came here three years ago to find a job, after selling off my flower business in the village,' he explained.

As he pedalled, Naseeruddin told me how, burdened by debt and unable to feed his wife and two daughters, he had decided to move to Gurgaon on the advice of a cousin who also worked as a rickshaw puller here. His cousin had loaned him some money to buy the rickshaw. Each month, Naseeruddin sent money home to his wife and daughters after keeping aside a paltry sum for his food and lodging.

'My wife Fatima tries to earn extra money by doing odd jobs in the village. Whatever she can get her hands on. My elder daughter, Nusrat, is eleven. The younger one, Chini, just turned five. Nusrat goes to a madrasa nearby but Chini is still young. She stays at home, helping her mother with her chores,' Naseeruddin sounded happy when he spoke about his family.

'I came here in search of a better life but it's very hard Didi. I barely make enough to make ends meet. People try to cheat me all the time. They travel long distances on the rickshaw and don't give me enough money. Everyone tries to take advantage of you when you are poor.'

It's a tough life. The man barely makes two hundred bucks in a day if he's lucky. The uneven Gurgaon terrain makes the job a strenuous one to boot. The rewards? Getting shortchanged all the time by people. I feel guilty and the fact that he comes from my part of the world only makes it worse. Is there anything I can do? Yes, for sure.

That is why I have allowed him to hire me! As his passenger, being carted to destinations I don't need to be carted to. I'm frowned upon and looked at with disdain by the Gurgaon women in their fancy cars. 'God, look at her, so tacky in that cycle thingy! Whoever uses those?' I can hear them snigger.

Can't say I blame them. Women like me (belonging to a particular demographic profile) don't really use cycle rickshaws in Gurgaon. They either drive their own cars or get driven around by their chauffeurs, husbands, boyfriends, brothers—depending on who is available and willing. In the rare instance when transport is not available and they have somewhere to get to in a hurry, they may use a rickshaw making sure that a battery of excuses is ready. Just in case they bump into someone they know.

'My car isn't back from servicing yet and my husband's taken his car to work.'

'Oh no, I bought a car yesterday but left the car keys in the showroom. They were sending it to me but I couldn't wait.'

'Both my cars are busy. I've bought a third car but it isn't here yet.'

'My kid wanted to go sightseeing in a rickshaw.'

The excuses keep getting more bizarre. There seems to be

an unspoken social code that people don't want to break. One must not be seen in rickshaws in Gurgaon. If you are spotted in one, people will automatically assume that you are economically challenged. Quite ridiculous, isn't it? But it's true.

Frankly, I couldn't give a damn. I choose my own mode of transportation. And while I'm perfectly able to walk (God knows I need that walk), and I own a car as well (and that's not an excuse) I'm not going to sweat it. If it's the small change that's making a big difference in someone's life, that's good enough for me.

Now where did Naseeruddin go? I need to make a quick trip to the grocers.

The shrill 'tring' of the cycle horn and there's a familiar voice behind me, 'Looking for me Didi? Hop on!'

5.

It's Not Halloween Yet but the Monsters Are Already Out

Negotiations for trick or treating during Halloween begin every year at our home around the end of September. Each year, my daughter begs and pleads that she be allowed to go from door to door, in the condominium we live in, asking for candies. Each year, my answer is the same— 'No.' Pleas become arguments which usually end in tears. This year, the tears have been replaced by a sulky silence.

You might think that I'm a harsh parent but Halloween is not a festival that is suitable for Gurgaon or even other parts of India. I don't like the thought of my daughter going to a stranger's house asking for candy. Who knows what kind of people she will run into? There are some nine hundred flats in our complex. I don't know each and every person who lives here. What if there is a pervert or a paedophile lurking in one of the flats? How will she protect herself? She's just eleven and a half.

Most of her friends are allowed to go candy-collecting. That makes it even worse. I become the demon, the Big Bad Mama in the general scheme of things. When I ask her if I can accompany her, she looks at me as though I have just escaped from a lunatic asylum. 'Are you serious Ma? Have you ever seen parents going trick or treating with their children on Halloween?' she replies, throwing me a scathing look. I remind her that yes, they do so abroad. But she's not prepared to listen. 'This is not abroad, this is Gurgaon,' she says. The negotiations reach a stalemate and we don't discuss it for the rest of the year.

There is a reason, however, why I write about this.

On a Sunday evening, while my daughter was tucking into her dinner in front of the television, another little girl, around the same age as her, was out delivering ironed clothes to the houses nearby. She was a dhobi's daughter, the washerman who operates out of a makeshift stall at a street corner, laundering and ironing clothes in the neighbourhood. A couple of hours later, my daughter was in bed, sleeping peacefully but the other little girl was dead. She had been raped, strangled and her lifeless body had been dumped in the bushes, like trash.

Every day, there are incidents of children being abused and killed in different parts of the Millennium City. A rape here, a murder there. Tiny paragraphs, tucked alongside the big screaming headlines, easily overlooked by people reading the newspapers. Most of these children belong to the underprivileged sections of society—children of servants, sweepers, cleaners, garbage collectors. They are mostly migrant workers from West Bengal, Bihar, Orissa and the Northeast who have come to Gurgaon in search of a better life—not very different from you and me.

A few days ago, the heavily mutilated corpse of a ten-year-old girl was discovered in a vacant plot near the rented home she occupied with her parents. The girl was raped, tortured and killed. The culprit had lured the little girl while she was playing outside, possibly with a bar of chocolate or a toffee. The savagery of the attack came to light when torture marks were found on her tiny body. The parents, impoverished garbage collectors from

West Bengal, were helpless. What could they do? Who would help them get justice?

There is justifiable outrage at how unsafe the Village has become, how we need to protect ourselves and our children from the monsters that have infiltrated our haven. The newspapers mention the drivers, conductors, migrant workers and the countless other people who have been spotted loitering around residential areas. There are stories about how the boom in Gurgaon's real estate market and subsequent increase in construction has led to an influx of people from all parts of the country, creating a law and order situation.

Inevitably, the finger of suspicion always points to those who are less privileged than us. Depravity and poverty go together, at least in our limited view of things.

I don't agree with that at all. What if it was someone like us, in both the cases? A monster living in a fancy house or a kothi nearby? Someone known to the girls, a regular client who lured her into his or her house? With something as innocuous as a candy. Have we forgotten what happened at Nithari? Sure, it was the servant who was charged with committing those horrific crimes. But what about the master of the house? Do you honestly expect me to believe that he didn't know what his help was up to? Weren't the unsuspecting children and women being procured for him?

In both these cases, the police seem to have reached a dead end in their investigations. I'm not surprised. Are they even looking in the right places? A couple of reports here and there and, in another couple of days, the newspapers would have lost interest as well. The girls will become another statistic denoting how unsafe the NCR is. The parents will be running from pillar to post to get justice. The culprit will be free, roaming the streets, luring more innocent children to their death.

My cook tells me that a man approached her on the main

road outside our condo the other day. He was good-looking and driving a fancy car. He told her that he needed someone to go over to his place to do some odd jobs. 'Hop on,' he said. 'My house is down the road. I'll drive you there.' When the woman refused, saying she would follow his car on foot if he drove slowly, he laughed and said, 'Are you scared? Do you know how much money I have? I can give you some of it.' To her horror, she saw that he had a duffle bag next to him with some bundles of cash inside. The poor woman was terrified. She turned around and fled. 'Did you get the car number?' I asked her later. She shook her head sadly. 'I don't know how to read and write Didi.'

It's not Halloween yet but the monsters are already out.

Now tell me, in a place as horrific as this, do we really need to celebrate another spook fest? A festival which teaches children that it's okay to be scary, one even gets rewarded for it?

Food for thought? Or would you prefer the candy that your child collected from trick or treating in the neighbourhood!

6.
Sadly Bengali

There are a zillion things about West Bengal I am proud of. That it has populated Gurgaon with its growing community of domestic helpers isn't one of them. In fact, this is first on my list of pet peeves at the moment.

Can you blame me? Look at what I have to deal with on a daily basis.

Everyone in the Millennium City has a maid from Bengal. So when I meet a person for the first time, the icebreaker always is 'Are you a Bengali? My maid is also a Bengali!' or 'I know some Bengali, I've learnt it from my maid.' Oblivious to the murderous look on my face, they go on, coyly testing on me the phrases they have learnt from their domestic help. 'Boshun, ashun, ...machh' and the mother of all phrases 'Aami tumake bhalobashee,' with a giggle. To that, all I want to say is 'Listen, I will smash your face with my wrist quite cheerfully if I hear that phrase one more time. Love is not to be trifled with!'

Then, there are those who want to be invited over immediately for a Bengali fish meal. 'Do you know how to make sorso machhi?' For your information, I don't even like fish. Arrghh.

My daughter has had similar experiences. She came home from school one day really excited after finding out that one of her new friends knew a smattering of Bengali. Thanks to the nanny, an import from West Bengal. Imagine my horror when I discover that the friend in question has learnt the choicest of slang from the nanny and is now using them with gay abandon at school. While no one else has the faintest idea what she is talking about, my daughter has decided to incorporate some of this colourful language into her sparse vocabulary.

'Son of a swine,' she yelled out loudly in Bengali the other day. She was writing an essay on my laptop and the lights went off suddenly.

'What did you just say?' I asked from the other room.

'This computer, Mama. It's the son of a swine,' she replied cheerfully. 'All my work is lost. I hadn't saved it and the computer got switched off because of the power cut.'

I nearly fainted. Thank heavens, there was no one else around. 'We do not use this kind of language in our home,' I told her sternly when I had regained my composure.

If this wasn't the pits, I also have to deal with people who believe that all Bengali Muslims are illegal immigrants from Bangladesh, responsible for the spate of crimes in Delhi/NCR. My neighbour Mrs Chopra is one of them. Each time she reads about a robbery in the newspapers, she comes running to my flat. 'Just see, these Bangladeshis are at it again. We really need to get rid of them from Gurgaon yaar!' Malda, Murshidabad, Dinajpur are not names they are familiar with, so I don't bother explaining. I don't waste my time. I'm beginning to realize that Geography isn't their strong subject either.

It's ironical that when I moved here, some 15 years ago, I found it thrilling that I could hire help and give them instructions in the mother tongue, not having to fumble with Hindi. For many years I laboured under the misconception that I was helping my community by providing employment to fellow Bengalis, offering some sort of leg up. I realized gradually that having a Bengali maid in Kolkata is a totally different ball game from having a Bengali maid in Gurgaon—a game I'm not particularly interested in playing anymore.

I've found that Bengali maids in Gurgaon prefer working for North Indian employers. I mean, it is North India after all. It's much more glamorous to have a Madam, rather than a Boudi to report to. Comparisons always creep in when you have Bengali help. They look at you as someone who has also moved to the chosen land in search of better prospects, and they resent the fact that you have gotten yourself a sweeter deal and they haven't. Nothing you say or do changes that.

Most days, I find myself desperately wishing I could hire someone who does not understand Bengali at all. Someone who doesn't smirk when I reprimand my daughter or take an hour to steam rice just so she can eavesdrop on me and my husband exchanging angry words. But sadly, whenever I spread the word that I'm looking for a maid, the ones that land up on my doorstep are always Bengali! They try to pass themselves off as North Indians, dressed nattily in salwar kurtas, confidently asking me, 'Kaam bali chai?' But I can always tell. Perhaps it's the shankha pola (bangles married Bengali women wear) or the vermillion smeared on their foreheads. Or the manner in which they struggle with the Hindi language. Like me!

Forget your own house, there seems to be no escaping the Bengali brigade even when you are outdoors. I have to be extra careful these days when I am shopping or inside a restaurant. The other day, a friend from Kolkata was sharing a juicy bit of gossip about her mother-in-law when I sensed that the waiter was hovering around our table, trying to eavesdrop on the conversation. When he caught me glaring at him, he volunteered sheepishly, 'Didi, I am from Calcutta!' As though that gave him the right to eavesdrop!

The fishmonger, the rickshaw puller and even the man at the stationery shop—they are all the same. With the same coy smile, there's the big reveal, 'Big Sister, I am a Bengali!' Ugh.

Some may not appreciate this aversion of mine since many of my dear friends in Gurgaon have Bengali maids they swear by. They should be glad that I've spared them the details of the other things about West Bengal I'm not proud of.

More about that another time!

7.

Sadly Bengali Again

'*Boobla, arektu mochar chop niye aaye tara tari!*' (Boobla, get some more banana flower chops quickly!) the lady seated at the table next to me shrieked out suddenly, giving me such a fright that I spilt some Coca-Cola on my favourite kurta. I glared at her. She glared back at me and I shrivelled under the force of that stare.

She was a big woman. Tall and dark, with frizzy hair that had been pulled back severely into a ponytail at the nape of her neck. She was sporting a gigantic pink bindi with a heavy line of vermillion on her forehead. She was wearing the ugliest pink brocade saree I had ever laid eyes on. The gold and pink on the saree hurt my eyes. So did the outrageous amount of gold jewellery she was sporting.

She seemed to be the matriarch of an equally loud family. There were at least ten of them—husband, children, aunts, uncles, cousins. Dressed in their Sunday best (if you count gaudy benarasi sarees and fussy lace dresses as Sunday fare), occupying a large table in one of Gurgaon's popular Bengali restaurants. There was a bottle of Champagne on the table, and the seniors were clinking glasses yelling, 'Cheeeears' while the children giggled and chewed on their straws and sipped Pepsi.

Boobla huffed and puffed his way back to the table, carrying two stacked plates of chops, spilling a few on the floor in the process. He didn't bother to pick them up, kicking them to one side with his feet. I think he was the matriarch's nephew. A tall man, Boobla didn't look a day over twenty-five, dressed in a blue striped shirt and navy blue trousers, having a slight hint of a protruding belly that all Bengali men past a certain age develop. His face was podgy and unpleasant with a thin moustache lining his lip.

Once he had dumped the plates on the table, he ran back to get some more. Replacement for the ones he had dropped on the floor. The matriarch yelled out to a waiter hovering nearby, asking him to get luchis (refined flour puris) for the children quickly. 'Make it as quick as you can. The children are very hungry,' she warned as though they were the only diners in the room.

They weren't actually. The restaurant was teeming with people. It was Poila Baishakh, the first day of the Bengali New Year, a day that is celebrated with much feasting and merriment within the community. Looking around me I realized that most of Gurgaon's Bengalis had gathered at this particular restaurant to eat lunch. The place was crawling with 'Booblas,' 'Babais' and 'Tumpas', dressed in brocades, benarasis, lace and chiffon. A young woman even had feathers in her hair! When I studied her closely, I realized that it was a feather-shaped object, possibly a hair clip, that she had fastened on her locks.

It was a hot April afternoon but I was beginning to feel underdressed in my kurta and jeans after looking at their fine clothes, jewellery and feathers. The waiters were running around like headless chickens trying to make sure the unruly crowd had a supply of fresh luchis, fries and miscellaneous fritters on their tables. I could hear the matriarch mashima's loud voice above the general din and piped Rabindrasangeet playing in the background. 'Boobla, ask the waiter for more fries!' A few of the children from their table had started running around in the aisles in between the seats. I noticed one of the waiters nearly tripping over them while hurrying to a table with a tray full of salad and papad. One blood-curdling yell from the mashima and they were back in their chairs again.

Traffic snarls had begun to form in front of the buffet table as people stood, stared and contemplated on the fare for minutes which seemed to stretch into hours. I realized that many of my fellow diners had no idea about how to eat buffet food. There is a particular manner in which one successfully negotiates the table. One has to be really quick. Take one stroll to determine what it is that you want to eat. Then, zero in on the dishes that you like, heap your plate with helpings and disappear. If there is a queue, you need to wait for your turn. You do not stand in front of the table blocking the others while you take your own sweet time to choose what you want to eat. It is a buffet table, not a shop window.

Sadly enough, my fellow diners that day didn't know or seem to care about following any etiquette. That they came from my part of the country even made it worse.

'Should I try the crab or the prawn, Mashima?' Boobla was standing in front of the buffet table staring at the spread. 'Eat both, I'm paying for it!' the matriarch mashima ordered. Boobla obediently started heaping his plate with generous helpings of both. 'I don't know why there aren't enough potatoes in the biryani,' she said loudly. 'Waiter! Why haven't you put enough potatoes in the biryani?' The younger nephews, nieces and grandchildren had surrounded her, blocking the rest of the diners from the buffet table.

I was hovering around patiently while all of this was on, hoping to sneak in and get some food when they were not looking. No such luck. The matriarch mashima elbowed me out of the way each time I tried reaching for a dish.

I'm not sure how we managed to get any food that afternoon. But we did, thankfully! I think the restaurant staff took pity on us and got us plates of luchi and fish fry so that we could eat something.

As we were walking out, I heard someone from the crowd that had gathered outside, waiting for tables to get free, whisper loudly in Bengali, 'Ufff, where do these non-Bengalis fly in from? Don't they have any other place to go? Why do they need to eat our food? They should go to a Dhaba!' Some others in the crowd sniggered.

Seriously? This is Gurgaon. This place belongs to the non-Bengalis. It's us who have flown in.

I'm not sure whether I should take being considered a non-Bengali an insult or a compliment. In the light of how obnoxious my community can be sometimes, I will take it as the latter! We need better manners, folks. I'm not sure which part of Bengal you come from, but I'm quite sure I have never encountered the likes of you growing up in Kolkata. I hope I never run into you again in Gurgaon either.

I'm sadly Bengali again!

8.
Gangnam Style

Beautiful, loveable
Yes you, hey, yes you, hey
Beautiful, loveable
Yes you, hey, yes you, hey
Now let's go until the end
Oppa is Gangnam style, Gangnam style

I was having a nightmare.

I had walked into my favourite café in the market next door for my usual fix of waffles with ice-cream and chocolate sauce. While the café looked the same from the outside, a strange scene greeted my eyes as soon as I stepped inside. There were Korean women everywhere I looked. They had occupied all the tables and were engaged in animated conversation. Some had wailing babies carefully placed inside colourful slings that were strapped on to their shoulders. Others were without babies.

Everyone looked the same—the women, the babies. There were plates of kimchi, bibimbap and bulgogi everywhere. There were no waffles, crepes or pastries in sight. A little hand was tugging mine. I looked down and my daughter had disappeared. A tiny Korean girl stood in her place, looking askance, mouth slightly open, braces showing, and had faded orange mehndi designs on her fingers and palms.

I screamed and found myself on my bed, tangled up in bed sheets, drenched in sweat.

When 2012 ended with Korean singer PSY's *Gangnam Style* becoming the most popular song on the Gurgaon partyscape, steadily replacing Mika Singh's boisterous melodies, I should have realized that something was stewing. That it would be a Jjigae or a Korean stew, I had no idea! Mulling over it now, I realize that all the signs were there. I had overlooked them. All the New Year parties I had the misfortune of attending, sooner or later, had switched to playing the loud, obnoxious song, which everyone seemed to love.

Not just that, everyone was familiar with the peculiar dance steps that accompanied the song—reminiscent of dancing cowboys getting ready to toss a lasso at someone. Can you imagine middle-aged Gurgaon people going through the motion? The entire spectacle was cringe-worthy, to say the least. I'm sure PSY would have disowned the song if he saw the dancing aunties with imaginary lassos in their hands, jumping away to glory.

But he didn't know and the enthusiasm of the local aunties was undeterred. There was just no getting away from that dreadful music. If you could call it music, that is. At home, it was pretty much the same story. My little girl was dancing to *Gangnam style* 24/7. More thumps, jumps and heavy-duty lasso activity. PSY had taken over my home too. Sigh.

Now it seems PSY and his ilk, upscale Gangnam residents, have moved bag and baggage to my corner of the world. Not content with taking over my home, they have invaded the Village, taking over my favourite coffee shops and restaurants. The ladies of Gangnam can give the ladies of Gurgaon a run for their money, dressed as they are in the most exquisite of clothes. There are days when I have to pinch myself to make sure I am in Gurgaon not Gangnam, Seoul. It's just a matter of time when crepes, waffles and pastries will no longer be served at coffee shops here. Instead there will be Bungeoppang, Chapssaltteok and Hwangnam bread.

I visited a fancy residential school on the outskirts of Gurgaon recently. Most of the children studying there were children of expats living and working in the Millennium City. After my work was done, the director of the school invited me to have lunch with him at the school lunch hall. At the lunch table, I found the attendants placing tiny ceramic bowls of kimchi on all the tables. When I looked at the director in surprise, he explained that the school frequently served Korean food, due to the large population of Korean students studying there.

'They are happy when they get home food. The school makes it a point to serve Korean cuisine at least once a week. Today's your lucky day!' the man was beaming from ear-to-ear when he delivered the last part of his sentence with a flourish. I realized that it wasn't just the students who were thrilled to be served Korean food, he was too!

I'm not surprised the school has so many Korean students. I hear there are nearly three thousand Koreans living in Gurgaon, who originally came to India on work or student visas. Most of them work for Korean companies such as Samsung, Hyundai and LG to name a few, and live in swanky condominium complexes across the Village. The children are sent to posh residential schools in and around Gurgaon offering the international curriculum.

I wonder if this is how the Koreans felt, all those years ago, when one of our own landed up on their shores on a boat. Talk about illegal immigration! And, from what I've read, they were quite hospitable towards her. Not only did they let her stay, she also ended up marrying a prince and settling there. I even hear they had twelve children!

According to the legend, Queen Hur Hwang-ok, also known as Princess Suriratna, was the princess of Ayodhya before she went to South Korea and married King Kim Suro of Karak Clan in AD 48. It is widely believed that she reached Korea on a boat and was the first queen of King Suro of Geumgwan Gaya.

There's a lesson in there somewhere for me. I guess it's all about embracing change. Like the Princess did, when she landed up in an unfamiliar land. Like they say in Korea, *Kwanyong-ŭn midŏk-ida. Kunja-e p'ilyo pulgagyŏlhan midŏk-ida!* (Tolerance is a virtue. For noble men, it is an essential and indispensable virtue!)

I've decided to spend the morning at one of the two new Korean bakeries at a neighbourhood mall. The bakery is the most delicious place I have ever come across. There are shelves stacked with bean jam buns, mozzis made out of Korean flour and red bean bread, fruit yogurt cream bun, assorted pastries and egg toast. They also have some fascinating fruit sorbets on offer. After that I'm going to eat lunch at Gung: The Palace. It's a Korean restaurant my friends have been raving about. I hear their food is rather good.

I've decided to be hospitable and embrace change.

Oppa is Gangnam style, Gangnam style!

9.
Modesty Is Back

I was getting ready for a dip in the pool when a woman wearing a wetsuit breezed past me. She was tall and slim, and she wore a black neoprene covering her from top to toe with a matching black cap on her head. I looked at her, astonished, because a wetsuit is a garment traditionally worn by people engaged in water sports, such as surfers, divers, windsurfers or canoeists. There was hardly any scope for exotic water sports in our handkerchief-sized neighbourhood swimming pool crowded by noisy bathers.

As I gaped, quite rudely, the woman headed straight towards the pool where she was joined by a few of her friends. Some of them were dressed in voluminous tent-like outfits while others were covered in billowy frills. I watched as they disappeared into the water minutes later, talking excitedly among themselves. They were not windsurfers or scuba divers, but merely Gurgaon women enjoying an early morning paddle, while preserving their modesty.

Swimwear, lately in the Millennium City, has begun to focus more on modesty rather than function. I would have gone a step further and said that this was something peculiar to our Village, but Nigella Lawson has changed my mind. The British celebrity chef emerged from the rippling waves in Australia's Bondi beach couple of years back all covered up in an eighty dollar black burkini leading many, including me, to think that modesty is back in fashion—on beaches and pool sides, spelling bad news for the oglers though.

The burkini is a bathing suit for Islamic women which covers the whole body except the face, the hands and the feet. France may have banned the burkini after the recent terrorism scare but it seems to be a regular feature in Gurgaon poolsides.

If you come over to my neighbourhood pool or any other pool in Gurgaon for that matter, you will find all manner of bathing suits on display. Bikinis, tankinis and even the humble one-piece suits are slowly making an exit from shop shelves here. Some of these so-called modest swimwear options are plain ridiculous in my opinion. I have no idea how serious swimmers can weave their way through the water with folds of cloth or frills weighing them down.

Aheda Zanetti, the Australian creator of the burkini, claims that she designed the bathing suit to give Muslim women freedom. How can anyone feel free with all that cloth covering them up?

My neighbour Mrs Chopra's pink-and-yellow printed bathing suit is the most ridiculous thing I have ever laid my eyes on. I can't look at the damn thing without erupting into hysterical giggles every time. The one-piece suit has a frilly skirt that covers the front and the butt region. Not just that, it has half sleeves which end at the elbows. It's really an eyesore!

'I don't know how you can wear that thing,' she said pointing at my navy blue bathing suit one day. We were at the pool for an evening swim. She had disapproval written all over her face when I emerged from the changing room.

'What do you mean?' I was puzzled. I was wearing a regular Speedo racer back costume.

'It's very indecent. Everyone can see the crotch and buttocks region in that suit. You should get one like mine. It will keep you well-covered. Mr Chopra would never have allowed me to step out wearing something like that.'

Well, I'm not married to Mr Chopra so I don't really care what he thinks. I didn't say this out loud to her, of course. I just laughed and changed the subject. If I didn't know her so well, I might have smacked the woman. But I know she means well. Besides, she isn't alone. Every second person I run into here is wearing a ridiculous bathing suit.

They insist publicly that the cover-ups are prompted by health reasons. Not everyone is as forthright as Mrs Chopra. Most of these women claim that they aren't really preserving their modesty. They are merely protecting their skin from the sun's harmful UV rays.

The people of the Millennium City have a phobia related to suntan. Every young girl, woman and aunty here aspires for a peaches-and-cream complexion. Even Mrs Chopra applies suntan lotion copiously before stepping into the pool with her frills. I've seen many women do the same. Not just that, they make sure their offsprings are oiled and greased before they get into the water. They are not particularly bothered about clogging up the swimming pool filters with grease from the oil. When it comes to priorities, a fair complexion is definitely more important than clean water.

Lawson had used that suntan excuse for her Bondi burkini episode. Her now divorced art collector husband Charles Saatchi liked all his women pale with alabaster skin apparently. Thank heavens she divorced him soon after. Though I secretly believe it was actually her vanity and a desire to hide her less-than-perfect figure (from all those midnight refrigerator raids) from the paparazzi.

Ditto for the Gurgaon ladies. They don't flaunt it when they haven't got it. The black neoprene is the perfect foil for the love handles and belly fat. I think the sun is just a convenient excuse.

Splash!

10.

A Sin to Tan?

A few days ago, my daughter and a few of her friends were splashing about in the swimming pool at the club across the road from my house. It was a balmy summer's day and I had offered to take the girls out swimming. Perched on a wooden bench with a book in a shady nook in one section of the club, I noticed that one of her friends was wearing a peculiar bathing suit. It didn't seem to be a bathing suit at all. At least, not like the ones I was familiar with. It was a fluorescent green t-shirt with black leggings to go with it. How odd, I thought to myself. Why would anyone wear a t-shirt in a swimming pool? My daughter and the rest of her friends were wearing traditional one-piece bathing suits.

I found out the reason just a few days later.

My daughter had outgrown the bathing suit she had been wearing (it had become snug in all the right places) so I had to go shopping in a hurry. I headed to a swimsuit store at an upscale shopping mall. There was a mind-boggling array of swimsuits on display—one-piece, two piece, tankinis, straight back, racer back. I must have been gaping at the suits on display wondering which would be suitable when I noticed a diminutive, young salesgirl hovering around. She had been following me from the moment I entered the store. I had waved her away impatiently on two occasions (I have a thing about salespeople following me around) but this one didn't seem to have gotten the hint. From the corner of my eye, I could see her spying on me from behind the clothes racks.

I felt my blood pressure rising, that familiar pop in my ears. I had decided on a sea-green one-piece suit after much contemplation and was getting ready to head to the cash counter to make my purchase and leave. It was then that I noticed the salesgirl shaking her head disapprovingly at me. She had moved closer while I was distracted.

Her name tag said she was Silky. I hadn't heard that name since Enid Blyton wrote the *Enchanted Tree* series. I wondered where Saucepan Man and Moon-Face were. I smiled to myself but she instantly took my smile to be a yes and started talking excitedly.

'Madam, are you sure you want to buy that piece? Come with me. I will show you something that would be more appropriate for you,' she beckoned towards the back of the store.

'It's not for me, it's for my daughter,' I said. But my curiosity, having subdued my annoyance, got the better of me. I followed her obediently to the back of the store, near the trial rooms. Perhaps there was something on discount I had missed out. I mentally reprimanded myself for being short with her earlier. 'Here madamji, look at these,' the salesgirl pointed to a rack on which hung t-shirts in different colours and sizes with matching shorts to go with them. 'These are very popular now. Everyone is buying them. They are good for the complexion.' I saw leg suits, tights and full-sleeved leg suits on the rack as well. I couldn't believe that I was looking at bathing suits for summer. They were similar to what my daughter's friend had been wearing the other day.

Had the girl just said 'good for the complexion'? I stared at her. What on earth was she talking about? 'Your daughter won't get a suntan madam if she wears this t-shirt instead of a swimsuit,' she explained. 'Now all the mothers come looking for these t-shirts rather than the swimsuits. There's so much sun outside and one has to protect the complexion no?'

When I'm really angry, I find that words fail me. So I fumed, silently, while paying for the swimsuit I had picked out initially. I'm quite okay with my daughter getting tanned while swimming. I don't feel the need to protect her complexion.

I couldn't resist getting the last word, though, while leaving the shop 'What about her face Silky? Do you have anything to protect her face from suntan? Like a mask or something? When she's swimming?'

Silky didn't have an answer, staring at me blankly. But I believe there is a solution. Women in China have been using masks to cover their faces when they go swimming at the beach to avoid getting tanned. I'm quite confident those masks will make an appearance soon at Gurgaon poolsides as well. There may be websites selling them as I write!

It all made perfect sense. I'd seen overzealous mothers slather on suntan lotion and sunscreen on their kids before pushing them into the water not bothering about creating an oil slick and jamming the filters in the pool. Even celebrity chef Nigella Lawson was ridiculed for wearing a black burkini (and looking like an oversized penguin) a few years back in Australia's Bondi Beach. Turns out she was trying to keep her ex-husband happy. He liked his women with alabaster skin. More suntan phobia. Eeeks.

I guess all is fair when you want your kids or your women to be fair and lovely. But is it a sin to tan? Or is it too complex a problem to solve?

11.

Nip Tuck and a Shot in the Butt

*Beauty comes from the inside.
Inside the salon that is.*

(Anonymous)

A group of us were hanging out at a close friend's home on her birthday last year when an argument broke out suddenly. One of the guests had casually remarked that women in Gurgaon were much better dressed than their counterparts anywhere else in India. Another woman (clearly belonging to the western part of the country) took umbrage to the comment and challenged her by saying, 'Absolutely not! Women in Gurgaon are very flashy. Women from Mumbai are much smarter and better groomed!' And it went on. During the course of the argument, many others jumped in, defending their territories, wagging their perfectly nail spa'ed fingers as they spoke.

I watched the action in silence. I didn't feel the need to defend West Bengal in matters relating to aesthetic sense. The new, spanking Big Ben in Kolkata (a replica of the tower in London) was proof of our good taste. Everyone knew that. I wished I was wearing something posher than my favourite pair of jeans and Anokhi kurta. Perhaps then, I might have been able to get in a word.

The way I see it, women from West Bengal may be smart but not necessarily smartly turned out. They don't stand a chance when it comes to women from this part of the world. The fancy ladies from Mumbai (I ran into a few of them during my last work trip) look jaded compared to their vibrant counterparts from Gurgaon—the ladies with Gucci, Prada and the designer what-have-you. These Gurgaon women had clothes and accessories fresh off the runways of Milan and Paris, impeccably coiffured locks, unblemished skin and sleek bodies.

Many a morning, when I roll out of bed and walk my daughter to school, I bump into some of these women. Not a hair out of place, flaunting toned bodies in sharp-looking gym clothes. One can't help but gape. In the afternoon, the hot pants and rompers come out and I fear for the lives of the drivers negotiating traffic on the busy road that leads to the school. In winter, there is the mink, fur, slinky overcoats and boots. It's like watching the pages of a fashion catalogue flip by in front of your eyes.

'Do you know a close friend of mine spends twenty grand at the beauty salon every month to make herself presentable?' a lady, sitting next to me, whispered at the party. I nodded. I could believe it. I know many women who spend obscene amounts of money to tidy themselves up each month. And you know what? I admire them for it. Instead of looking like something the cat dragged in, these women take pride in themselves and their appearance. What's a couple of thousands when you can end up looking like Ms Universe. Sorry, I meant Ms Gurgaon.

Nip and tuck, teeth whitening, skin polishing and the latest thing doing the rounds—buttocks. Yes, you heard right. Buttocks! It's the latest fashion in Gurgaon I hear. I had nearly jumped out of my skin when the beautician at the salon helpfully advised me to try some to look younger.

'Why don't you try some buttocks then Madamji?' the young girl enquired politely when I asked her if she could suggest a remedy for my dry skin.

It's one thing to be told you have yellow skin. Yes, I have suffered that too. But when someone tells you that you could do with some buttocks, that's just outrageous. My buttocks were just fine, I thought to myself angrily.

'Excuse me?' I said out loud, glaring at her angrily. Was she making a pass at me? An inappropriate suggestion perhaps? I squirmed uncomfortably in the leather chair.

'Buttocks madamji, you should try some buttocks!' she repeated politely as though she had just asked me to try a new flavour of tea.

I could feel myself turning purple; there was a familiar choking sensation at the base of my throat, ringing in my ears.

The girl hadn't noticed and droned on, 'It's the latest thing in Gurgaon. Try it. It will make your face look younger.'

My mouth dropped open in astonishment. Make my face look younger? What on earth was she talking about? It sounded like a bizarre plastic surgery experiment—taking skin off my butt to make my face look young. The girl smiled, 'Oho Madamji it's nothing to be afraid of. It's not painful at all. I have many ladies taking these "buttocks" injections.' She explained that they would remove my old age lines and make me youthful again. I still couldn't figure out what she was rambling on about. Injections in my butt to look younger? How was that even possible?

And then it finally dawned on me. It was not my butt she was interested in rejuvenating or using skin from it to make my face youthful. The girl was pushing for Botox shots—an extremely lucrative side business, no doubt.

All that smooth, baby skin I saw on the women all around me suddenly made sense. They were using 'buttocks'. Lots and lots of it.

Relief washed over me but I couldn't stop giggling hysterically for many days after that. I didn't go back to the parlour for a while. I needed time to think. There was a lot at stake.

All my life, I've been indoctrinated in the virtues of simple living and high thinking. Well, whoever coined that phrase (and I have a strong hunch it was Mahatma Gandhi) has clearly not lived in Gurgaon! Here you are only as good as you look.

I think it may be time to try that shot after all!

12.

The Other Monkey in My Life

Ooh-bitchdoo, I wanna be like you
I want to walk like you, talk like you, too
You see it's true, an ape like me
Can learn to be like you, too

(The Monkey Song, *The Jungle Book*)

Monkeys have taken over my life. Literally.

No, I'm not talking about the ten-year-old and forty-something-year-old I share my apartment with.

I woke up this morning to find Dunston stuffing a banana down his throat on my balcony. Now my balcony isn't just any other balcony. It is the pride and joy of my life. There are wrought-iron planters neatly arranged on one side, which hold my prized collection of potted plants. There is a Fabindia dhurrie laid out in the centre with a small cane stool and table on it—the place for my early morning tea and reading.

Dunston was perched on one of the cane planters that held my plants, his gigantic, hairy butt squashing the delicate pink and white flowers that had just bloomed. As I watched in horror, he proceeded to finish his snack, turning around to gaze at me once or twice dismissively. Before he jumped over to the next balcony, he flung the peel rudely at me. It hit the glass with a loud thwack and landed on the floor. A broken terracotta planter lay nearby as tragic evidence of his visit. The planter was one of my favourite purchases from a weekend bazaar in Delhi.

In the distance I could hear the muffled announcement on our building's Public Address system. An announcement that strikes dread in my heart every time I hear it. 'Please keep your doors and windows locked, a monkey has come into the complex. Please do not offer any food!'

Offer food? Had the guards totally lost it? Like I would say to Dunston 'Care for a banana?' when I would spot him on the balcony and roll out the red carpet. What I didn't know, however, was that residents did offer them food. Devotees of Hanuman ji. I could see some of them moving about in the surrounding flats getting ready with their offering of bananas and sweets.

Grumbling to myself, I sped around the house, trying to secure my doors and windows.

Come bug season each year and it becomes 'planet of the apes' all over again. Where's James Franco when you need him? Held to ransom inside the house as hairy, four-legged beasts go on a rampage, wreaking havoc outside. If you think I'm exaggerating, come live in my house pre-Diwali and you'll know what I mean. A family of monkeys camped on a friend's terrace for a week once. After they were done, it took her a month and a small fortune to get the place cleaned and looking as pretty as it did before.

I've changed houses twice because of the monkeys!

In my first Gurgaon house, a tenth-floor apartment in a condominium, a strange noise outside the main door one evening had led me scurrying to the peephole to make sure it was not burglars. Those were my early days in the Village. Our building had a handful of residents and our floor, only us. Squinting, trying to adjust my vision through the tiny gap, I could make out a blurry shape on the floor, huddled near the wall, picking at stuff from the floor and putting it into its mouth. It looked like a child. I yelled out to my husband in alarm. 'Oh my god, someone's left a baby outside and it's eating things off the floor!' My husband took one quick look through the peephole and exclaimed, 'That isn't a child, that's a little monkey eating bugs on the floor! All the noise from the crackers must have driven it up here.'

I soon found out that the child had a family—a mother and a father. Each night, they would have a bug fest outside my door, sorting the bugs into three neat piles. One for Papa M, one for Mama M and one for Baby M. Every morning, when I opened the door to get out of the house, I would find three neat little piles of leftover bugs (saved for the next evening I guess). I would shout out to the sweeper, tell him to clean the area at once. But, the piles would reappear the next evening. And so, my life went on like that. From one pile of dead bugs to the next, till we moved.

The next home, alas, was closer to the ground and near a park. There were monkeys everywhere! In twos, threes, even twelves and thirteens. It was *The Jungle Book* all over again with King Louie's subjects. Unruly gangs that danced on our terrace and drank from the water tank. Danced on our Maruti and broke the rear window. Stole clothes from our clothes racks and attacked the maid when she came in with a grocery bag. She never came back to work after collecting money for her tetanus shots! Can't blame her.

Every morning I would find an article of clothing from a neighbour's house decorating the bushes in front of our gate. A blouse, a shawl, leopard-striped lingerie. Ugh. Whatever they could lay their hands on.

My daughter was a couple of months old then. With a baby

at home, I was terrified to step outside. A neighbour 'helpfully' informed me that monkeys sometime steal babies, and not just clothes! I was on guard, twenty-four hours of the day. I was living Aung San Suu Kyi's life.

I was so happy when we moved again. Little did I know that my happiness would be short-lived.

Dunston checked in again. Over the last ten years, he's pretty much been the other man in my life. There's simply no getting rid of him.

13.

Neither Shaken nor Stirred

'Mama, can you feel an earthquake?' The thirteen-year-old comes running to the kitchen. I am busy cooking Sunday breakfast. I look up from the pan and tell her, 'Could be. But there is no way I am leaving the building without eating the bacon that I am frying right now.' She looks exasperated, shrugs and then leaves.

Before you get ready to hand me an award for my composure in the face of disaster, let me tell you that it wasn't always like this.

I can't imagine sleeping peacefully through an earthquake or snoring contentedly while the ground rumbled and shook beneath me, sending people into a tizzy. But for the first time in fifteen years, I have been able to do that. And I can't tell you how happy that makes me. So relieved that I almost feel like celebrating with a vodka martini, not shaken or stirred! It's almost as if I've cheated fear itself, fear that I've been living with, ever since the very first earthquake I felt in Gurgaon.

Chamoli, 29 March 1999
Having moved to Gurgaon from Calcutta a year back, we rented a quaint apartment on the tenth floor of one of the oldest condominiums in Gurgaon, Silver Oaks. Life was all about work and hectic after-work partying. After a particularly bohemian night

with friends, alcohol and loud music, we had collapsed into bed a little before midnight. Just as I was floating into a dreamless slumber, I was rudely poked by my husband from his side of the bed. 'Stop shaking the bed,' he growled menacingly, speech still blurry from all the liquor. 'Stop shaking the what?' I got up angrily, ready with a stream of abuses to hurl at him for disturbing my sleep, 'I'm not shaking the...' but before I could finish my sentence, I noticed our cane bed shaking rather violently. I looked up, the fan was swaying this way and that. My heart skipped several beats. From the next room, I heard my brother shout out, 'Earthquake, run for your lives!'

Easier said than done. Getting dressed in a hurry and running down ten flights of stairs is no easy task. Especially when you have gallons of alcohol inside you and your vision is blurred. But we made it, and heaving for air in the open parking spaces next to the building, I wondered why we had bothered to race downstairs at all. If the building did fall, we would be buried right under it. I made a mental note to stay properly dressed at all times, even at night. Several of the residents who had gathered downstairs were gawking at my Snoopy night suit.

Kutchh, 26 January 2001
After the first earthquake, I grew restless. I would look at the fan a lot, just to make sure that it was not swaying. The aftershocks ceased in a few days but I often felt my head do a little spin randomly. I would get hot flashes at the thought of another earthquake. Nightmares of being trapped under rubble. I started looking for excuses to get closer to the ground.

Then Kutch happened and breakfast was never the same again. From getting ready to tuck into a nice, hot breakfast of scrambled eggs, toast and bacon to running down (you guessed it) ten flights of stairs again! I had to get out of the damned tenth floor flat, and fast.

In the years that followed, I moved houses—a two-storeyed house, facing a park. Life was peaceful, earthquake-free. Though there were pests of other kinds. That's just the thing about life. The grass is never green enough! My daughter was born, we got burgled and it was time to move again.

Only this time I insisted that I would not move higher than the third floor if I had to live in a flat again. It's no joke running down ten or twelve flights with a baby in your arms. With Gurgaon being a seismic zone, I was not taking any chances this time. We moved into a fourth floor flat in another condominium and I started getting my earthquake kit ready. Just in case. It consisted of packets of formula, water, odomos, flashlight, wallets, credit cards. Strangely, the list kept increasing and the bag got heavier. How on earth would I lift it if we had to leave in a hurry? We started going to bed fully dressed at night. Our shoes, bags and earthquake kit were neatly stored next to the bed. We were all set.

Days passed, months even. The milk powder started smelling rancid, I started digging into the earthquake kit and using up the supplies when I felt lazy to shop. Soon the (empty) bag disappeared under the bed. We started getting into bed in our disreputable night wear, tired of being poshly turned out all the time. Our wallets and bags went back to being scattered all over the house, in places you would never find in a hurry.

And then it happened in the dead of night during winter. After a New Year's party at a friend's house. As we raced down the stairs, with our five-year-old, desperately trying to avoid being trampled over by neighbours, we couldn't stop cursing ourselves. Huddled in our car, near an open field, a little distance away from our block of flats, we sat in silence, angry and fearful while our little toddler kept lisping cheerfully at regular intervals, 'Is this an earthquake? Are we going to die?'

Neither Shaken nor Stirred 51

Her optimism in the face of natural disaster kept our spirits up. We didn't die but all three of us caught a dreadful cold from sitting out in the freezing cold for over an hour. We were laid up for nearly ten days and let me tell you, it wasn't fun. My earthquake kit reappeared again with fresh supplies and I made a vow never to touch it again.

I kept my promise, and the kit is still there under the bed, intact with bottles of musty water, sour milk and expired medicines. In all the earthquakes that followed over the years, whether at night or in the afternoon, I have never been prepared or remembered to grab the kit before leaving the house. In the most recent one during the summer last year I think, I rushed down only to realize that my t-shirt (which I threw over my camisole in a hurry) was inside out! Nonchalantly, I walked up and down the park as I waited, pretending as though this was the latest style, ignoring the curious stares and sniggers. Gurgaon women are always well-dressed, even in times of calamity. I am the only exception to that. Though I once saw a woman wrapped in a towel trying to hide behind a pillar. Poor soul!

The moral of my story? Don't know if there is one. It's hard to be prepared for an earthquake and after years of fearing them and trying to stay alive when it happens, I sleep through them all now.

Oh well, until next time I guess. Till then, I guess I should go check on that earthquake kit. Something has been smelling foul under the bed!

14.

Holy Cow

$\mathcal{I}$ nearly lost my life in a pileup the other day.

The auto I was travelling in, to get home from work, was speeding along as usual despite my repeated warnings. 'Don't worry Didi,' the driver told me cheerfully in Bengali as he negotiated the turbulent evening traffic, 'You are safe in my hands.'

Turns out, I wasn't. No sooner he said this, he pressed his feet on the brakes abruptly and the auto came to a screeching halt. I was thrown violently against the metal rail that separated the driver's seat from where I was sitting. I heard the sound of splintering glass, screeching tyres and a raucous medley of car horns. 'What happened?' I asked the driver weakly, rubbing the part of my stomach the rail had pushed into. The driver popped his head out of the auto and back in again. He told me that we had crashed into the car in front of our auto, which had braked suddenly and had crashed into the car in its front and well, you get the picture. That's how pileups generally happen.

Turns out a family of cows had decided to cross the road right in the middle of the busy thoroughfare leading to the crash. The matter would have ended if the cattle had swiftly crossed the road and got to the other side without delay. But they were cows not humans. Somewhere in the middle of the road, they decided to stop, sit and ruminate on the world at large. That is when chaos erupted.

I got out of the auto nursing my injuries which included a scraped elbow, a sore tummy and a bump on my head and stared at the creatures lounging on the road. They stared back at me, steadily and insolently. One of them even shook its horns at me and said, 'Moo!'

People for the Ethical Treatment of Animals (PETA) say that cows have feelings and they hold grudges against other cows who treat them badly. Now I've been called a cow at various times in my life. My angry mother, frustrated brother and sundry other people have used the word on me to express their dissatisfaction with the way I behaved. So believe me when I say that I know exactly how cows feel. At that very moment, I didn't really give a damn that they would get upset because I, another cow, had called them names. They certainly deserved it, holding up traffic like that.

I cursed them soundly (under my breath) in my mother tongue as I didn't want to get into trouble with the law. They take things like that very seriously in the Village. Seeing that the auto was in no shape to complete the journey, I paid off the chap and walked the rest of the journey home.

Cows are God's own creatures in Gurgaon and the rest of Haryana. In the early '90s, blue cows or nilgais were spotted grazing in this region, at the foothills of the Aravallis. The nilgais have long since disappeared, in their place, one sees white cows. Lots and lots of them. But you can't curse them or do anything inappropriate to them. They are allowed to hold up traffic anywhere they like, stray into private properties, eat plants and flowers from your garden and not be fined for it. Not just that, you have to treat them with way more respect than you treat your own mother. Garland them, offer prayers to them and as tradition dictates, offer the first roti to them.

Sally, my colleague from Canada had been following this tradition faithfully for years. Only she had no clue that she was indeed following it. Married to a North Indian, she was tired of the rotis that her mother-in-law made for her. Morning, noon and night. For every meal. So she went up to her room, like an obedient daughter-in-law, and flung the rotis out of the window, eating the packed sandwiches bought from a local deli instead. She had become quite a favourite with the cows grazing in the empty field next door to her house. They were having a field day, every day!

When I told her that she was actually following Indian tradition in the most bizarre of ways, she giggled. 'Good heavens! Thank god you told me that. At least my mother-in-law won't be annoyed if she found out what was happening to all those rotis. I'm actually feeding the other mother, gau mata!'

It's good to feed your cow mother, but one shouldn't entertain thoughts of eating her. Just as you wouldn't eat up your own mother, you shouldn't be eating your cow mother either. So don't even think about biting into a juicy steak while you are in Gurgaon. Rare, medium or well-done. Steak is taboo here in the Village and other parts of Haryana as well. We aren't that modern yet! Cow slaughter and sale of beef are punishable offences and you can be jailed for anything between five to ten years. In fact, the local government is also planning to impose a gau seva tax on the sale of alcohol in the Village.

I wonder if the gau rakshaks are aware of the traffic situation caused by the cows today. This self-appointed army of cow protectors guards the cows ferociously, making sure they aren't abused, smuggled or harmed. I'm sure they would have rushed to the spot and escorted the errant cows safely back to their shelters, built at various villages in Haryana. There are some shelters in

Gurgaon too I hear. I've also heard that the punishment meted out to offenders is quite stern, like being forced to eat cow dung for their misdeeds. Eeeks. I hope no one heard me cursing the cattle!

With all the attention the cows are getting, they may well become our national animal replacing the tiger. In any case, one wrong syllable and Gurugram can easily turn into 'Goru' Gram ('Goru' meaning cow in Bengali).

God help us if that happens. Imagine writing that as an official address.

Holy Cow!

15.
Brawn and the Beautiful

Beefcake is back in fashion in Gurgaon. And I'm not talking about a new dish in the fancy foreign restaurant that's just set up shop!

At a recent lunch outing, a few of my friends started gushing about Aamir Khan's hot bod in the movie *Dangal*. The conversation soon moved on to Bollywood hunk Hrithik Roshan and his bulging pecks. 'I wonder whether we will see his awesome body in his new movie,' some of the ladies cooed. By the time the pad thai noodles and the green curry had reached our table, the ladies had moved on to the third hot bod John Abraham and how he had disappeared (taking his hot bod along with him). 'What a shame!' my friend Sonali rued, dousing her bowl of noodles with green curry, 'that delicious body has gone to waste. He needs to start acting in movies again yaar!'

I'd have been happier had they been talking about a new dish in the fancy foreign restaurant. Or steaks. But that is taboo in Gurgaon.

Shaking my head exasperatedly, I tried (in vain) to reason with the ladies. It's not that I dislike Aamir Khan. I admire his histrionic skills and the effort he put in to look like a professional wrestler in the movie. I just don't understand what it is about brawny men that gets our knickers in a twist. Hadn't these women heard the saying that all brawn and no brain makes Hrithik a dull boy? Well, they hadn't and didn't want to either. So I ate my noodles in silence, mostly, not missing an opportunity to sneak in a clever comment whenever I could.

Hrithik reminds me of Johnny Bravo, the heavily muscled hero of a hugely successful animated TV series for Cartoon Network. My nephews were crazy about him and after hours of babysitting I got hooked too. Bravo had a pompadour hairstyle, an Elvis Presley voice and tried picking up women with his cheesy lines—'Enough about you, let's talk about me, Johnny Bravo. Wanna see me comb my hair, really fast?'

Despite his good looks, Johnny Bravo never got the women he wanted. None of his lines worked. He would get roughed up and the women would walk away. He cut a pathetic figure. Strangely enough, like his cartoon avatar, Hrithik's physical strength doesn't seem to get him the girl either! His fairytale marriage with Suzanne ended disastrously some years back. Soon after, news of a secret fling with a Bollywood actress made headlines. Things turned ugly and the two had a public spat. After a fair bit of mudslinging between the two, the romance ended in disaster. He had no wife, no girlfriend. So much for his washboard abs. I'd say they were a complete washout.

My friends didn't agree, dismissing my reflections as hogwash. They went on and on about Aamir, Hrithik and John, adding more brawn to the list as the hours wore on. I sighed as I got the lowdown on the beautiful bodies of Tinsel Town.

While the Bollywood beefcake heroes can be switched off with one click of the TV remote, there's no escaping the real-life Johnny Bravos in Gurgaon these days. At shopping malls, grocery stores, even at the doctor's chambers! There's an overdose of brawn all over the Millennium City.

Just the other day, I ran into one. We were all huddled together in the tiny reception area of my doctor's chamber waiting for the doctor to materialize. Mr Brawny walked in with his girlfriend Ms Slinky. He looked so much like Johnny that I had to stifle a giggle. He gave me a cold stare. No 'Hello Mama,' for me. The young lad, he wouldn't have been more than 26 or 27, looked as though he may have gone slightly overboard with the chest press and the dumbbells. And, those arms...they would have put Popeye's nemesis, comic book villain Bluto to shame! His red shirt was a size too small. Buttons open. Chest, clean shaven. Green trousers and tan loafers on his feet without socks. What on earth was he thinking?

Ms Slinky could have done with some more clothes. Her leopard print tights and flimsy top were clearly not enough to ward off the December cold. So she kept clinging on to Mr B for warmth. Not that he minded. I noticed how all the women in the tiny room sat up with interest when Mr B walked in. Including the hunched old grandma who sat in the corner with a walking stick for support. All of a sudden, everyone was fiddling with their hair, fixing their clothes and eyeing Brawny interestedly through the corner of their eyes. The grandma in the corner was sitting up straight. It was a miracle. Brawny was completely unaware of all the female attention on him. He had eyes only for his girlfriend, which should be a good thing. But their public display of affection was making me really uncomfortable. I'm an old-timer. I don't really do well with public displays. Thank heavens for my smartphone. Touchscreens can come in handy when you need to fiddle around with something to look busy.

The doctor arrived soon enough and theirs was the first appointment! I heaved a sigh of relief. They didn't seem to be married to each other. I couldn't help but wonder what they were in for. Could he have gotten her into trouble? The way she was fawning over him, it couldn't have been a cause for aggravation anyway.

Why are women in Gurgaon attracted to such an obvious display of masculinity? In Drona's Gurugram, rippling muscles and bulging pecks may have signified power, masculinity, sexual virility or dominance but we've left those days behind, haven't we? Intelligence, quick thinking, wit—aren't these the qualities women admire in men? Women don't want to be overpowered or dominated anymore. Or do we?

16.
Fifty Shades of Grey

I've been hiding from my hairdresser. It's complicated and involves copious amounts of hair dye.

Let me tell you about my hairdresser first. He's a bit like Zohan from the movie *You Don't Mess with the Zohan*. If you haven't watched it, that's absolutely okay. I'll tell you all about him.

Zohan is an Israeli counter-terrorist with a ridiculous accent who is a natural when it comes to styling hair. His sexual prowess also makes him somewhat of a hit with the ladies who queue up for haircuts at the salon where he works. Well, for haircuts and other things!

My hairdresser is from Rohtak and he's not a commando. He is far from it, in fact. He's a meek version of Zohan and I like to refer to him as Mohan (A meek Zohan). I have absolutely no idea what his real name is. He might have told me once but I've forgotten. Haryanvi accent aside, he's extremely good with hairstyles. Tell him what you want and he almost always gets it right. I'm not sure about the sexual favours part. He's never made a play for me. I haven't ogled at him either. Though I've seen many aunties give him the once over at the salon. Many Gurgaon aunties are like that.

Besides, I'm hardly anything to make a play for. I'm forty plus, married with rapidly greying hair and an expanding waistline. Mohan seems to think there's great potential though. He's always recommending the fanciest of styles and treatments for my thinning hair. Too bad he doesn't have any potential. Not in my eyes at least. He's painfully thin with acne on his face and the most horridly hennaed cowlick in the middle of his forehead.

Now the young fellow has been pestering me for months to cover my grey hair with some hip and happening hair colour. Each time I saunter into the salon, located in the neighbourhood market, he rushes over, makes me sit down in one of the many leather chairs, inspects my scalp and makes a face, 'Madamji, what are you going to do about all this grey hair? It's getting worse. Tsk tsk tsk!'

I have figured, from his disapproval, that it's not cool to be a greying woman in the Village or anywhere else in India for that matter. 'Have you noticed how many hair colour adverts are aired on television Madamji?' he says. 'Why do you want to look old?'

Poof! There goes my secret ambition of looking like Nafisa Ali. In this life, at least.

'*Madam, aap ooomberrrr shade try kar lijiye, aapka yellow complexion ke saath achha lagega!*' he declared a few weeks ago when I had popped in for a customary shearing. I stared at my reflection in the mirror in horror. Yellow? Why did he think I had a yellow complexion? Was it my weak liver? And what in God's name was ooomberrrr? Was it a Haryanvi version of amber? Fibbing that I was in a hurry because I needed to pick up my daughter from school, I fled as soon as he had snipped off the overgrown bits of hair. 'I'll come back soon for the hair colour, I promise.'

I lied.

The first thing I did when I got home was look up the meaning of the damn word. Turns out it was ombré, a French-termed

62 *Gurgaon Diaries*

hair trend featuring darker, more natural hues at the roots with gradually-dyed lightening at the ends. Apparently many A-list celebs such as Jennifer Hudson, Naomi Campbell, Rihanna have been spotted sporting the look. While I'm flattered the young man thought I could carry such a fancy look, obviously these A-listers are not on the wrong side of forty with yellow skin.

The ombré look is quite popular with many A-list celebs in Gurgaon as well. I run into many of these ladies in my daughter's school and at parties flaunting their ombré locks. The Page 3 in the newspapers are plastered with their pictures too.

My grey hair has been giving me sleepless nights. To dye or not to dye, that is the question. Should I age gracefully or try my hand at being a hip Gurgaon mom with aplomb, oomb... sorry ombré or blonde? Blondes do have more fun, even if they are obese with a liverish pallor. I've been looking at hair colour catalogues (on the sly) to help me decide, but I've been getting more and more confused.

Unable to deal with all this dithering, my daughter has taken the matter into her own hands, providing some much-needed perspective. She, like the Duchess of Cambridge, feels that grey hair is befitting a mother. Who can forget Kate's grey hair pictures splashed all over British newspapers when she was pregnant. 'Remember, Mama,' my daughter warned me the other day when she caught me wistfully looking at hair colour charts online, 'with great dye comes great responsibility.'

True that. It's a huge responsibility. I just don't think I'm ready to be a hip Gurgaon mom yet. Ombré can wait. Sombre is in, at least for me. I've decided to hang on to my greys for a wee bit longer.

Until it's time for my next haircut! I'm going to dye another day.

Fifty Shades of Grey 63

17.

Things That Go Bump in the Night

Or should I say people who are neighbours.

Ever since I can remember, I've been living in various condominiums across the Village with some really strange people, who did strange things at night. They'd play catch with a dog or move furniture around with a *bumpity bumpity bump* or grind masalas using a mortar and pestle at 2 a.m. There was also one bloke whose father-in-law ran the entire length and breadth of his living room at night. Every night, without fail. I'm quite sure that he was insane. He lived right above us.

Last night, I heard someone banging on the recently-installed LPG pipeline in our building. The metallic *clang clang clang* at regular intervals kept me awake the whole night. I couldn't spot anyone from my balcony when I looked out. The entire complex was shrouded in black. When I asked the night guard this morning, he stared back at me in dumb amazement. He hadn't heard any noise in the night. The whole thing was so mysterious. Ghostly even.

You will understand why I haven't had much use for an alarm clock in all these years. Why use an alarm if you didn't get to sleep at all?

I'm wondering if I'm slowly morphing into the crazy French

lady at 101/103. Let's just call her Isabel C here.

I had just moved to Gurgaon from Kolkata. We were living in a rented apartment in one of the few condominiums that were around those days. Our two-bedroom flat had a breathtaking view of the brown, undulating Aravalli terrain dotted with trees. There was a quarry out front and on a clear day, one could see the blue airline sheds at the Delhi airport.

I would be all alone all day long in the empty flat while my husband was at work. I'd unpack furniture and go through job advertisements in the newspapers. Since there wasn't much furniture to unpack (we were just starting out, having gotten married a couple of years back), there was hardly anything to do other than watch the telly and read. We had lots and lots of books.

I had started on a brand-new Ruth Rendell one evening when I heard a knock on my door. It soon turned into banging. Loud and insistent. I dropped my book nervously and ran to the door. I couldn't see anything through the peephole, the corridor outside was dark. My well-meaning relatives from Kolkata had warned me about the dreaded Aravalli dacoits that burgled homes in this region. What if the dacoits were outside? I opened the door ajar, safety lock still in place, and peered into the darkness, heart beating like a drum.

'Stop ze banging at once!' an angry voice yelled at me. It came from somewhere near my knees. I looked down in surprise. Once my eyes had adjusted to the darkness, I saw a lady, tiny and stout, in her fifties probably, with silver grey hair, glaring at me. 'Stop ze banging I warn you,' she yelled again. 'You are deeesturbing me!' There was a steely glint in her baby blues.

I blinked and gasped at her. Banging? What banging? I was only reading my book. Besides, there wasn't anything to bang on. 'I didn't make any noise,' I attempted feebly. She waved her hands in the air, rolled her eyes theatrically and said: 'Deeedn't make ze noise? What nonsense are you talking about? You make ze noise every evening. I can't bear it anymore!'

I could feel tears pricking my eyelids. Those days, I would cry at the drop of the hat. Typical Bengali sentimental fool that I was. The Gurgaon aggression hadn't made its entry yet. When I think back to those days, I can't help but think how ridiculous the whole situation was. She was so small, I could have stepped on her. But I was cowering instead.

'I didn't bang anything,' I said to her again, in a louder, more forceful tone. 'Besides, we have just come from Kolkata, there isn't anything to bang here. We hardly have any furniture!'

The crazy lady stormed off in a huff, muttering in French.

It happened again a few days later. This time, it seemed as though she would break down my door. And she wasn't alone. There was a burly Bihari security guard fidgeting uncomfortably next to her. He looked apologetically at me and said, '*Yeh madam ne aapke bareh mein complaint kiya. Please aap awaaz mat kijiye. Inko disturb hota hai!*'

I stuttered angrily and started in my faulty Hindi '*Arre disturb hota hay ka matlab kya hai?* I am the one getting disturbed. This silly woman is breaking down my door and saying that I am making some kind of noise. I am not making any noise. What will I make noise with? Please come inside and see. There's no one at home and we hardly have any furniture.'

The guard looked at Isabel and waved for her to enter my house. She stepped inside with the guard following closely. I watched from my vantage point by the side of the front door while she went from room to room, inspecting. After a couple of minutes she had returned to the living room which was empty save the rickety cane three-seater in one corner. She walked over to where I was standing, shamefaced.

When she spoke, I noticed that her voice had dropped several octaves and she had tears welling up in her eyes. 'I'm so sorry I've troubled you. I can see that you are not making ze noise. But every evening, I hear sounds coming from above. Someone moveeeeng furniture, dropeeeeing zings. It is troubling me.'

She explained that she had moved here from France because she believed it was better (and quieter) to live in Gurgaon rather than Delhi. She was a writer and did some volunteer work at a local orphanage in her spare time.

'I have no idea who could be making those sounds,' I explained. I could make out she was batty. I had been living in that apartment for the last two months and there were no noises in the evening, loud or otherwise. In fact, the solitude was eerie at times.

I bid her adieu, promising to drop in for some chocolat chaud à l'ancienne soon. I never did. I don't think you can blame me for that. I can't help but wonder what she would have done if she had my luck with neighbours. It would have probably resulted in a nervous breakdown.

Though of late, it seems as though the God of Good Neighbours has decided to bestow His grace on me. High time I think! I've suffered silently for nineteen years. My new neighbours are both polite and quiet. They are never seen or heard except during Christmas when they emerge from their flat bearing gifts—neatly packed packages of bacon and sausages—for me. They own a cold cuts company in Manesar, an hour's drive away. I return the favour with a freshly baked fruit cake. We don't see each other again for the next 365 days.

Thank you Lord. Give us our yearly cold cuts and forgive us for our sins. Amen!

18.

Lost in Translation

'*Yeh rosshogolla keetna kaurke hai?*'

The elderly, bespectacled lady next to me had directed the question to the boy behind the counter. She was wearing a crisp gold and green cotton saree, reeking of expensive perfume, white hair pulled back into a bun. She looked at me suspiciously, through her steel-rimmed glasses, when I smiled at her. 'Are you a Bengali?' I asked politely, reaching out for my box of sweets neatly packed and waiting on top of the counter. She did not look pleased. 'How did you know?' she barked.

Seriously, I thought to myself, as though there was any doubt after hearing you speak in Hindi!

'It's your saree,' I offered instead. 'It's a Dhaniakhali isn't it? It's very pretty!'

Dhaniakhali is a village in West Bengal famous for its handloom sarees. She grunted and went about inspecting the other sweets on display, ignoring me completely. I sighed and walked out of the shop. I could hear her telling the boy, '*Mere liye yeh kalo jamun pack kar do!*' What an unbelievably rude woman, I thought to myself.

On the way back home, I noticed an irate Bengali mom yelling at an autorickshaw driver who was blocking her child's bus in front of our condo. '*Hum tumko peeeeetai kaurega!*' Hell hath no greater fury than a language-challenged Bengali mother whose child can't get on to the school bus. The auto screeched to a halt in the middle of the road, nearly crashing into my car in the process, did an abrupt about-turn and fled in the opposite direction. Can't say I blame him. The woman was squealing like a banshee.

Bengalis in Gurgaon! As much as we like to pretend otherwise, our Hindi isn't terribly good. Of course, the ones born and brought up in Delhi or other parts of North India do not count. Their fluency and grasp of the Hindi language is impeccable. Just like it should be. But lesser mortals like myself—direct imports from West Bengal—struggle with the language, often with hilarious consequences.

I still remember our early days in Gurgaon. Trying to make sense of our strange new milieu as we set up house. Trying to fit into an alien landscape devoid of people and languages we were used to. The shopkeepers hardly spoke English. We hardly spoke Hindi. How would one communicate? There were so many things we needed to buy—groceries, commonplace household objects, etc. Things we had no names for in Hindi.

The nigella seeds that we use to flavour Bengali fish stews and vegetables are called kalo jeere in Bangla but what on earth did the Haryanvis call it in Gurgaon? Did they even use the seed? How would I even explain what I was looking for? So I figured the best way to find out would be to call my family back home. They didn't have a clue. 'Why don't you try kala zeera?' a few of them offered helpfully. Unfortunately, that wasn't the name at all.

For years, I struggled in my kitchen without using the seeds till I made friends with a few Bengalis from this part of the world. 'Arre it's called kalonji!' they told me, amused to hear my tale. 'I can't believe you hadn't been able to find the right word all these years.'

'No I hadn't,' I said. We celebrated that evening with a delicately flavoured fish curry, liberally sprinkled with kalonji!

The cobweb cleaner was another thing that caused us great grief. In West Bengal, cobweb cleaners are called jhool jharus. Loosely translated, that means a cobweb broom, a particularly long piece of bamboo with a broom attached to its end. You can point it towards the ceiling and brush away cobwebs with ease.

After a couple of cursory visits to the stores in the Millennium City, I noticed that there wasn't anything remotely resembling a jhool jharu in sight. There was a mind-boggling variety of brooms and mops, in various shapes and sizes, all fancy shmancy. I was completely at a loss. When I would try describing the damn thing to the shopkeepers in English, they would just stare at me blankly. That's when I decided it was safer to come home and consult my husband first before I spoke to the shopkeeper again and displayed my ignorance.

'I'll get it for you,' my husband declared when he got back from work and I told him about my problem. 'I know what it's called. You don't need to worry!' Impressed by his confidence, I joyfully got into the car with him as we raced towards the store to buy our cobweb cleaner. Inside the store, my husband walked up to the shopkeeper (with a slight swagger) and said, *'Aap ke paas jhool ke liye baaans hoga?'*

The shopkeeper, an elderly man with spectacles, stared long and hard at my husband. Oh, if only I could describe that look. After what seemed like eternity, he turned away and said, *'Yaha jhool wool ke liye koi baans nahi milega!'*

That was the end of our shopping expedition. The cobwebs would have to wait.

19.
Time to Change

'These clothes are ekzaaktly right for my body types!' the lady exclaimed loudly before rushing out of the trial room, her face hidden by the huge pile of clothes she was carrying. I heaved a sigh of relief and rushed into the empty room. I had the room to myself at last.

I had been waiting patiently for the last half an hour for one of the five doors to open so that I could have my turn and try out the outfits I had picked out. It was a Sunday afternoon and the upscale clothing store at Ambience Mall—a swanky mall in the Millennium City—was packed with shoppers. Mothers, daughters and aunties stood in queue in the narrow corridor waiting, just like me.

I slammed the door shut, anxious to get on with the unpleasant task at hand. To be quite honest, I find the process of trying on new clothes physically taxing and emotionally draining. Huffing and puffing, trying to squeeze into garments in a cramped space, oceans of sweat running down the body. The discovery that one is overweight and the clothes just don't fit despite expert manoeuvring leads to weeks of depression. Life would be so much easier if one could just pick things off racks and make them fit. Like magic.

Enough daydreaming, I reminded myself sternly. I had a job to do and time was limited so I got busy. Just as I had removed the last article of my clothing and was getting ready to squeeze into a sexy black number, there was a series of rude knocks on the door. Startled, I called out, 'Yes?'

The lady on the other side of the door was yelling in Hindi. I'm going to attempt to translate some of it for easy reading. The parts I understood, that is. 'Arre,' she screamed, 'My clothes are in there! I hadn't finished trying on clothes. I had just gone out to get some more blouses in different sizes. How can you walk into the room when someone's clothes are still there?'

I put my glasses on in a hurry and looked around the tiny chamber. In one corner of the floor lay a knitted top that I hadn't noticed earlier. I picked it up. It didn't look new, had no tags attached to it so clearly the lady on the other side of the door had left it there. I bundled it up and pushed it out through the opening under the door. There was no way I was going to open the door, undressed as I was, and give her the top. What if she pushed me out of the way and captured the room again? 'This is the only top in the room so this must be yours,' I said stiffly.

'You should not have walked into the room,' she continued. She had the most annoying voice, high-pitched and whiny. 'I had left my blouse so that I could come back. Now all the rooms are occupied and I have to wait for a long time till I get a chance.'

At this point I completely lost my temper. I had given her a patient hearing despite her rude behaviour but there was a limit to which my patience could be stretched. Besides, I did have serious anger management issues.

'You can't leave an article of clothing behind and block a room,' I sputtered in rage from behind the door. 'Once you have finished trying on clothes, you need to leave so that someone

72 *Gurgaon Diaries*

else gets a chance. If you need to try on some more clothes, you have to wait for your turn like everyone else. I'm sorry but that is how it works. Have you seen the long line of people waiting for their turn? I suggest you join them.'

She stomped off, heels going *clickety clack*, but I could hear her arguing with a salesgirl in the distance. 'This is not done,' she was saying. 'She should not have walked in. How can you go into a room when someone's clothes are still there? I want to speak to the manager right now!' I couldn't make out what the other woman was mumbling and to be quite honest, I didn't really care anymore. I had managed to get inside a trial room and I was going to make the most of the time. Let her go ahead and call the manager. Let her call the police for all I care, I thought to myself.

After a couple of minutes, when I could no longer hear her voice and it seemed safe to come out, I did. The diminutive girl behind the counter at the entrance to the trial rooms was apologetic. 'Ma'am, I'm very sorry,' she said, eyes downcast. 'This happens so often and we really can't do anything.'

I gave her a patient hearing. Poor thing, it wasn't really her fault. I realized that this was something that happened very often at upscale stores in the Village. Women, even men, kept their clothes behind in the trial rooms while they shopped around in the store so that the rooms were booked for them, whenever they chose to waltz in with clothes to try on, for hours and hours on end it seemed. Sometimes, they left their mothers or elderly aunties to guard the rooms so that no one could enter! The store managers were usually reluctant to step in and settle these disputes as they didn't want to lose their customers. Also, because they were scared. Some of these women were really obnoxious.

I learnt that day that changing room etiquette took on a whole new meaning in this part of the world.

So the next time you go shopping for clothes in Gurgaon,

Time to Change 73

remember to carry some old clothes with you or better still, an ageing relative, to reserve your spot in the trial room. Else be prepared to wait for hours and don't say I didn't warn you.

As for me, I'll just carry an empty shopping bag. The hard plastic ones. I find these bags quite effective in settling disputes.

Whack...thunk!

20.
Kids off the Menu

I was about to pop the chicken and chive dumpling into my mouth when I felt a pair of eyes on me. Turning around I saw a toddler, standing next to our table and looking at me with a decidedly ugly, bordering on malevolent stare. I froze, dumpling hung in the air. The toddler came closer and poked my stomach with her chubby little fingers. As I flinched and moved back, the dumpling fell on my lap with a splat. She then turned her attention to the can of Coca-Cola on the table and tried pulling it towards her. 'Coca, Cola,' her lips were mouthing the word, soundlessly.

I find that the older I get, the less maternal I become. I prised her fingers (gently) from around the can and pushed them away. The little girl seemed to display superhuman strength and wouldn't budge an inch. She shook her curly head and stamped her feet. Her beautiful grey eyes welled up with tears and her mouth trembled a little. Was that the start of a tantrum? I looked around helplessly.

Where, in God's name, were the parents?

The upscale Chinese restaurant, in one of Gurgaon's new malls, was teeming with diners at lunchtime. There was no sign of the missing parents. All of a sudden, a girl, no more than fifteen herself, came running to our table out of nowhere and picked up the stray in her arms. The stray was in the middle of a violent tantrum, not having gotten the Coke from my table, thrashing her hands and legs wildly. The teenage nanny had another little boy in tow—the stray's brother. He stared suspiciously at me and then turned away to look at his sister with interest as she proceeded to scream the house down.

The teenager looked ashamed, hair dishevelled, wearing a shabby t-shirt and denims. She hurriedly mumbled a few words of apology in Hindi. From the look of it, she had been distracted looking after one while the other had gotten away. I nodded, unsure of what I was supposed to do. She hurried back towards a table at the far end of the restaurant and I spotted the parents (finally) eating lunch, quite unaware of the commotion their offspring had caused. They didn't look up from their meal and I'm quite sure they hadn't even noticed that one of their children had gone missing. The nanny skulked around, looking rather uncomfortable while the children ran around the table, squealing in glee.

For the next one hour, the maid (slightly older than my own daughter) walked up and down the length and breadth of the restaurant keeping the little brats busy while the parents finished their leisurely lunch. I couldn't help but stare at her, my own meal forgotten. At one point, the little boy started wailing uncontrollably and she had to rush to the washroom with him, the girl hanging onto her legs for dear life. Not once did the mother get up and offer to help. She just went on eating as though that was the most normal thing in the world for her to have done!

Perhaps I'm being slightly drastic but don't you think restaurants in India should ban ill-behaved children and their parents? If you can't look after your own children when you are out, perhaps you would be better off eating at home. And it's not just me. There are many people who don't enjoy children running wildly in the aisles of restaurants, dodging waiters carrying heavy plates of food. Kids shrieking and crying is not my idea of piped music. Keep the volume down, for heaven's sake.

Besides, I find it really uncomfortable eating food in the presence of maids (who are mostly children themselves) walking around looking after other children without being given any food to eat. It makes me very sad and that does not constitute an enjoyable dining experience for me. Why on earth should I feel guilty for something that is not really my fault! If I'm paying for a meal at an expensive restaurant, don't I have the right to be able to enjoy it without having noisy, ill-mannered children ruining it for me or an overactive guilty conscience, for that matter. So if you can't mind your children or your manners, why not stay at home instead?

There was another incident when I spotted a woman outside a reputed British pizzeria in Gurgaon. She should have stayed at home with her spoilt little brat. The overweight boy was having a tantrum, shrieking shrilly, 'Mummy! *Mujhe yeh Pizza Hut ka pizza chahiye!*' The lady, barely in her twenties, was trying her best to get the boy away from his chosen spot blocking the entrance of the restaurant. The brat refused to move and I had been forced to gently push him aside so that we could head indoors.

Now, I'm not normally impatient but I don't have much tolerance for children having tantrums. It's best to leave them alone and move on. Leave them at home? And if you feel bad about it, stay back yourself perhaps.

21.

Fat and Loving It

For the umpteenth time. No I don't run and I don't jog either.

On a good day, I can barely crawl out of bed, hobble across to the kitchen and make myself a cup of tea before dawn breaks and all hell breaks loose!

Don't even ask about the bad days. Trust me, you don't want to get there…

I'm the red mark on Gurgaon's lean, mean landscape, a rather round peg in a square hole.

Denizens of the Village are passionate about fitness and good health; everyone from your friendly neighbourhood uncle to the grandma across the hall. If they don't walk, they run or jog or do exercises whose names sound like tongue-twisters. My neighbour's kitty party group does yoga in the park across my house. Each morning, as I drink tea in my balcony, I spot Mrs Chopra, Mrs Majumder and Mrs Malhotra sprawled on yoga mats in the grass doing impossible things with their arms and legs. I see many men hanging out of their balconies as well, waiting to catch a sight of well, erm, you know what.

It wasn't always this way. I too had nurtured a secret ambition to morph into a lean Gurgaon aunty but a series of unfortunate (mis)adventures at local gyms have completely put me off exercise.

In fact, even the thought of making eyes at Milind Soman recently couldn't get me into a pair of track pants and on the track with the other runners in the Village. The dishy model was in Gurgaon last year to raise funds for cancer through a run for charity. Gurgaon's gorgeous, sleek, svelte moms were all over him. Lucky them. I went green with envy looking at all the pictures on Facebook.

I guess, you could say that I'm officially 'over the hill'. Not that I was ever under it.

In school I was the girl who was always the last one standing, when teams for games were being picked. Did I mind? Nope. Anything remotely connected with sports or exercise was never my thing.

You may be thinking that being a Bengali girl, dance was my passion. Nah! That was not happening either. In fact, the only time I showed some movement at my Indian dance class in school was when a caterpillar found its way from the tree on to my skirt. I wriggled, I shook, I shimmied in a desperate bid to get the damn thing off my uniform. Needless to say, my dance teacher was not impressed. 'Stop clowning around,' he had admonished. 'If you are not interested in dancing, you can go back to class!'

Now, years later, as an overweight forty-something, things don't seem to have changed much. Sports and fitness still don't seem to be my thing. Not that I haven't tried. I'll tell you about my adventures at the gym another day. I tried out a treadmill at a friend's place and ended up spraining my ankle on it. That put me off machines altogether.

Yoga wasn't an alternative either. The anorexic girl who landed up on my doorstep claiming to be a yoga instructor took one look at me and disappeared. In a way, you could say that exercise has shied away from me. And I've never cared. Until now.

With festivities around the corner and the promise of cutlets, chops, fries and biryani, I am suddenly racked by guilt pangs. I'm wondering whether to take this as a good sign. A sign that there is hope even for a sinner like me. Yes, gluttony is a sin, didn't you know?

Hang on a second. Guilt pangs don't originate in the stomach, do they? My tummy just growled!

Looks like it wasn't guilt after all. It was hunger! There I go again.

22.

The Ghost in the Machine

Elevators make me uneasy.

This has nothing to do with the fact that I watched a horror flick last night that had five people stuck in an elevator with the devil among them.

And no, a certain ponytailed editor's recent sexploits with his colleague inside one has nothing to do with it either.

You see, elevators can be terribly unpredictable pieces of machinery. It wouldn't be wrong to say that they seem to have a mind of their own.

The other day, an elevator came hurtling down several storeys in our condominium, completely of its own accord. There was a little boy and his maid inside. They were going to a birthday party in an apartment on the third floor. The maid pressed the button to get to the third floor from the tenth. The machine decided that it would head straight down to the ground floor instead. No stops along the way. Thankfully, the duo inside were not hurt but were dreadfully shaken I would imagine. And while I have heard varying accounts of the incident, it's clear that the wires snapped.

Given the pressures of modern living, people are snapping. Why not elevators I say? They have to endure years of misuse, neglect and odious people. And dogs. Who love to pee inside the compartments! Heck, I would have snapped if I had to put up with all that.

Dogs are regular users of our condominium elevators. Not that I mind dogs, I'm actually quite fond of them but I find it slightly uncomfortable to be travelling in an elevator with one. They are usually all over the tiny space, with their tongues hanging out and god forbid if they have to do their business.

Last month, I got stuck inside an elevator for what seemed like several hours. In reality, it was probably a couple of minutes before the damn thing started working again. Thankfully, I was alone so no one could see me make a complete spectacle of myself as I turned grey and hyperventilated. Oh, did I mention I have claustrophobia?

Remember the old-fashioned elevators with metal collapsible grills that you could open to get in and out? Those were a safer bet. You could always prise open the grills and climb out in case of an emergency. I've done that plenty of times.

The modern metal tins are the pits. Tins are for sardines. Not real people. Automated tins give me the creeps. And where did all the liftmen go? There's something really disturbing about being in a machine that might be a malevolent one. Or being stuck with the devil.

Do you think I might have watched too many horror sci-fi movies?

Whatever it is, I wouldn't want to be at the mercy of an intelligent machine having a bad day. I don't fancy being suspended in mid-air, stuck or crashing down a shaft locked in a can.

Our condominium has recently had some fancy lifts installed. Schindler's Lifts, no less. They have black steel walls and a faux marble floor with piped music playing as you ascend or descend.

On second thoughts, I think I'll take the stairs instead!

23.
Pesky Pigeons

The more I read about cows, the less sense it makes to want to kill them, leave alone eating them. Besides, I live in Gurgaon. It's politically correct to want to leave them alone. I don't want to be in the bad books of some 'Gau Rakshak'. I've heard they make people eat cow dung as punishment.

An article that I came across on the People for the Ethical Treatment of Animals (PETA) website recently described cows as 'diverse as cats, dogs and people. Some are bright; others are slow learners. Some are bold and adventurous; others are shy and timid. Some are friendly and considerate; others are bossy and devious.'

The article went on to say that cows are similar to humans, capable of interacting in socially complex ways, developing friendships over time and sometimes holding grudges against other cows, who treat them badly.

That's when it struck me. Hell, I could be a cow. And I wouldn't want to be eaten rare, medium or well-done with either mushroom or mustard sauce drizzled on top. Would you?

So why are we getting all hot and bothered about the government's ban on cattle slaughter? It might be a good thing after all. The cows will thank you for abstaining.

PETA says that cows mourn their dead and separation from loved ones. They even shed tears. Believe me, you don't want to incur their wrath or bring on the waterworks. A cow chased me down the road when I was little (God knows why) and that traumatic episode has lived on in my memory forever.

So I propose that we stop killing cows and eat pigeons instead. Grilled, roasted, any damn way you like. I don't really care.

The feathery monsters have made my life a living hell and it would be really nice to see their tribe decrease. From taking over my balconies, defecating on my beautiful flowers and freshly laundered clothes to setting up cosy nests in air conditioner vents, they've done it all. To top it all, they have also managed to reproduce successfully despite my ominous presence in the zone. I can hear their demonic spawn cheeping away to glory in the mornings.

Unfortunately for me, the condominium I live in is infested with bird lovers. I'm quite okay with them really. They can do all they want in the privacy of their own homes. They can keep the feathery beasts in cages inside their living rooms, gazing and cooing with adoration the entire day. What I'm not okay with is throwing bits and scraps for the pigeons to feed on from your balconies, which then land on other people's balconies and make their lives a living hell.

Like mine for instance. The lady who lives above me has been chucking dried pieces of roti and bread for days leading to a mini-Trafalgar-Square-like situation in my balcony. But even Trafalgar Square got rid of its pigeons. It's time for me to do the same. Perhaps I need to get a pet hawk.

Most days, I find myself obsessively searching for 'helpful hints on how to get rid of pigeons from your home' on Google. I have tried everything but nothing seems to work. I have filled a spray can full of water and run out screeching obscenities, spraying water all over the place each time I've spotted a bird or two. I've scattered paprika powder and pepper all over the balcony. The Internet says that pigeons hate spices. But while I've been sneezing like crazy, thanks to the spice overdose, the pigeons don't seem to have budged an inch. Flap, swoosh! I can hear them flapping outside the window again!

I worry that someday, if I'm not careful enough, they will take over my house. If you hadn't guessed it already, they've flown off with my sanity! It's about time that we left the cows on the street (where they belong) and turned our attention towards these feathery fiends.

Celebrity chefs Nigel Slater and Jamie Oliver have some interesting pigeon recipes. Apparently, the birds taste best when grilled or braised. From casseroles to sandwiches, there's every kind of pigeon dish for your plate. Take your pick—Pigeon and Peas, Pigeon Breast with Cherries and Walnuts, Flying Steak Sandwich. I can so see myself lounging in my bird-free balcony with one of those, a favourite book and a glass of wine in hand.

Game on!

24.

Sweet Memories

It's all very well to be living next door to a French bakery. To walk past shop windows decorated with colourful macaroons and exotic pastries, smell of fresh bread wafting through the doors. All fancy shmancy. Or a chocolate boutique with boxes of designer chocolates stacked up high at the entrance, signboards advertising the delicious goodies on offer.

As I grow older and my Bengali genes establish their dominance, I seem to be moving further away from designer fare and yearning for the simple, earthy pleasures of my childhood.

Not that Gurgaon is lacking in any respect. Fancy malls, designer stores, spas and restaurants, you name it, the Village has it. Too bad there aren't any mishthan bhandars around. 'Deshapriyo,' 'Sarvopriyo,' any damn kind. I'm done with antiseptic sweet stores where blank-faced sales staff weigh and wrap sweets in plastic gloved hands. Shiny counters, shiny floors don't seem to impress me anymore. The human touch is conspicuously absent.

The other day I was shopping for sweets in a sweet shop near my house. An old relative had dropped in unannounced and I had to make an emergency trip to buy some sweets while the rest of the family kept him entertained at home. The shop was spanking new with a white signboard outside that said 'Bengali

Sweets Sold here'. There was nothing remotely Bengali inside.

I saw a huge expanse of shiny floors (that you can eat out of) flanked by neat glass shelves on either side in which various sweets were displayed. I noticed that there were some containers on top of the counters with different coloured sweets stashed in them. I gathered they were placed there for the customers to sample before they chose what they wanted to buy.

There were some interesting looking orangey squares piled on top of one of the containers. I reached out to take one.

'Excuse me! What are you doing madam?' I saw a man behind the counter looking at me crossly.

I flinched and pulled my hand back. 'I want to taste that. Aren't those for tasting?'

'Yes, they are for tasting but please don't touch them with your hands. Please ask me and I shall give you what you want to taste,' he reprimanded me. I was amazed at his rudeness.

'In that case, you need to put a signboard for customers that says they must ask your permission before they can touch the sweets. How is one supposed to know?' I said nastily.

He stared at me coldly, shrugged and moved away to attend another customer. I wasn't offered an orange sweet to taste.

I felt humiliated, my cheeks turning beetroot red. Instantly, I did not feel like buying anything from the shop anymore. I turned around and walked out in a huff.

The experience has left me yearning for the sweet shops of my youth. They had grimy interiors, sticky floors, wooden chairs and rickety tables where you could stop for a bite. Not that we were ever allowed to. A yellowed, stained basin at the corner would be placed where people could wash their hands. A friendly voice would ask *Didibhai, ki debo?* (Little sister, what can I get you today?) As you got older, it would become 'Boudi,' 'Mashima' or 'Dida' depending on your age bracket.

The kind of shop where you could choose your favourite mishti (danadar, gujiya or kalo jam) by pointing to stacks of sweets neatly arranged in the glass box. The already dirty glass would mist if you went too close. The sweets would be weighed and neatly wrapped in small cardboard boxes held together by rubber bands. The ones drenched in syrup would be packed in a bhar (earthen cup) covered by a sheet of greaseproof paper held together by rubber bands! They would be called gartar (read garter) by the shopkeeper. Heaven knows why!

There would be a dubious, wobbly cake-like thing on a stand on the counter, with flies buzzing around, with a slice or two cut out of it. I later learnt that it was something called a milk cake. Really wonder what it tasted like. We were never allowed to try it. The flies must have been a big deterrent for the adults accompanying us!

When I was little, I often wondered why my youngest uncle (who lived in France) would demolish platefuls of steamed rice and posto when he was visiting us for the holidays. He would hardly touch any of the fancy fare that was offered to him. Day after day, posto and rice was all he ate. Till it was time for him to fly back. 'How boring,' I would think to myself. 'He lives in France. Why does he go crazy about this kind of plain food on a holiday? Uggh!'

It's taken me some thirty years to figure out the answer to that question. You never realize the value of a moment till it becomes a memory.

25.

Freedom Calling

Freedom means different things to different people in the Village.

For my young domestic helper, freedom has come in the form of a cellphone, recently purchased from a second-hand shop somewhere close to the jhuggi where she lives. Chaina is barely 23 years old. She got married off by her parents when she was sixteen years old. Having left her three children with her extended family in her village in West Bengal, she has now moved to Gurgaon in search of better prospects.

Chaina is tall and slim, with frizzy, brownish black hair that she ties loosely into a bun at the nape of her neck. Her eyes sparkle with mischief on some days, thin lips curved into a mysterious smile. Other days, her face is drab and lifeless, mouth set in a straight, mirthless line. I notice that the pallu of her shabby printed saree covers her head when she lands up for work each morning. Once indoors, the pallu is flung back and her head remains uncovered for the rest of the time.

'Didi, are you listening to me?' she is standing next to my chair holding a shiny black purse in her hands. The purse has a bejewelled red Apple logo on it. She has taken the phone out of the purse and is waving it under my nose. I can see the plastic cover on the side peeling off.

'Look Didi, I can click pictures with it,' she says excitedly. 'It even has the Bengali alphabet,' she points out.

I try to look interested, putting down my cup of tea and the morning papers on the table to glance at her new, old phone. Her eyes are glittering and the face is alight with joy. Her enthusiasm is infectious and I find myself struggling to appear aloof.

'Give me your number so that I can call you,' I say. 'To find out where you are when you disappear from work sometimes!' she ignores the mock reprimand. Instead she giggles. 'Yes, now you don't have to call my husband anymore,' sticking out her tongue at me as she disappears into the kitchen.

I watch her, out of the corner of my eyes, as she finishes all her household chores over the next one hour with a spring in her step. All of a sudden, a discordant melody fills the living room. The new phone is ringing. The girl rushes to her purse and fishes it out, walking into the kitchen for privacy. I can hear her whispering angrily. 'I can't come home now, I have two more houses left to clean.'

Over the next couple of months, I notice the excitement dissolve into despondency. Gone is the spring in her step. Most days she can barely drag her body to work, worn down by some invisible weight. The purse is gone. In its place is a faded plastic bag.

'Are you feeling well?' I ask her one day. She's dusting the piano, bending over to wipe the bronze pedals clean. She looks up at me, wan faced. 'I'm fine Didi, nothing is wrong with me.'

'Really?' I prod. 'You don't look okay to me.'

She stands up, fixes her saree and bursts into tears—loud, wracking sobs. I'm taken aback by the suddenness of it all.

'Why are you crying, silly girl?' I tell her awkwardly, not sure what to do. 'Tell me what the problem is at once.'

In between sobs, she tells me that her husband has decided to return to the village. The odd jobs he was getting were not enough to make ends meet or sustain his alcohol addiction. With Chaina unwilling to leave with him, he was also threatening to marry someone else.

'He's taken away the phone now. Says coming here has turned my head,' she cries, leaning against the wall. 'I don't want to go back to the village Didi, I hate it there. There's no freedom at all. I am cooped up at home all day looking after my in-laws. I'm not even allowed to talk to anyone. I will surely die if I'm made to go back! But what can I do? I don't want to lose my children.'

It all made sense now.

For her husband to have allowed her to have her own phone was a big step. I had seen her dishevelled and morose at work sometimes. I was positive now that he abused her as well. Over the last six months that she had been working for me, I had suspected that he was a controlling man, limiting her access to most things.

The gift was a bribe for her acquiescence. The moment he had realized that she would not return to the village without putting up a fight, he had taken it back.

Isn't it funny the things we take for granted? Our independence for one.

That day when she left to go home was the last I ever saw of her.

26.

Irritable Bowel Syndrome

'Are you quite sure?' the woman on the other end of the line was insistent. I could sense that she wasn't about to take no for an answer.

'Yes, I am. Quite sure,' I said firmly. 'You are wasting your time with me. I don't need them. Perhaps you can try calling someone else?'

There was silence. Good grief! Why doesn't she hang up, I thought. It was ten in the morning and I had my writing to get back to. My head was swimming with ideas and the tele-caller was making a huge nuisance of herself.

'Who doesn't need bowels in their house? Everyone needs bowels!' she shrieked. A final sting at me before she slammed the phone down.

I couldn't have argued with that logic. Everyone does need bowels in their houses.

Back where I come from, bowels are an inescapable reality. They make exciting breakfast table conversation, to be had with cupful of piping hot tea and singara (samosa) or dry toast, if they haven't been particularly cooperative, that morning. The bowels, that is.

Bengalis love their bowels and they never let an opportunity pass when it comes to a stimulating bowel discussion. Throw in some telephone brand Isabgol or milk of magnesium and you have a winner!

Hadn't someone famously remarked once that when a Bengali comes, can the bowels be far behind? No, Bengalis and their bowels are a killer combination indeed. Much like luchi (puris) and cholar dal (chana dal), we love talking about bowels, functioning or otherwise. Even with strange women who randomly call early in the morning.

But my lady caller couldn't have known that. She was just happy that she had finally found someone who had taken an interest in her bowels. And interested I was till I discovered that they were not real.

They were plastic with pretty pink flowers on them. 'Just like the British royal family has,' she giggled.

Something was just not right.

'Plastic? With pink flowers?' I gasped.

'Everyone likes designer things these days,' she explained. 'So we copied the British design. And you don't need to worry. You can put these bowels in the microwave. They won't melt. You can even pour hot kadhi in them. They will be just fine. Not a scratch. Buy a set, you won't be sorry!'

I knew the Royals were tough but microwave proof bowels with pretty pink flowers? That would put even a self-respecting Bengali to shame. I could feel my bowels wince at the very notion.

Turns out, the woman wasn't about to take no for an answer. She called up again, a couple of days later. By a fortuitous twist of fate, this time I was not at home. My mother, however, was. The 75-year-old picked up the phone and was greeted by the same breezy voice asking for me. When my mother told her that I was not home, the tele-caller asked my mother whether she was, in fact, my mother.

'Yes I am,' mother said.

'Hello Auntyji, I have a wonderful offer for you. Today is your lucky day. You have been chosen as the recipient of a free set of bowels!'

Before I tell you what happened next, let me also tell you that my mother has recently recovered from a prolonged and painful colon surgery. So she was not particularly overjoyed when someone offered her bowels over the phone. That it was free made absolutely no difference to her!

How did the conversation end? Let's just say the woman won't be calling us for a long while.

She's figured that our family has a case of the Irritable Bowel Syndrome.

27.
Hellish Symphony

My neighbours, the Chopras, have installed a fancy new car alarm. Every time someone walks past the car, a thousand roosters start crowing all at once, in synchronized ear-splitting harmony.

'What on earth is that sound?' I shout out in alarm. It sounds worse than the earthquake warning siren they've installed in our building recently.

'Isn't it cool?' Mrs Chopra gushes. 'It's our new car alarm. We chose the one with the roosters. They remind my husband of his home in Punjab. "Kukkad shukkad" and all that!'

I have no words.

If I ever ran into the man who invented car alarms… Let's just say that for his sake, I hope I never do!

4 a.m. every morning, for the last nineteen years in the Millennium City, it's been the same.

Waowwaowaowaowao

Pickapickapickapickapicka

Aooooooooooooogaaaaah

And now, with the Chopras' new toy, a new sound—*Cock a Doodle Do Cock a Doodle Do Cock a Doodle Do*.

And I'm up, blurry-eyed and raggedy-tailed, rudely awakened at the crack of dawn by the bizarre medley of sounds, originating from various car alarms set off by car washers in my condominium as they go about their daily business.

'Can someone turn the damn thing off? Deactivate it at once, you morons!' I scream from my balcony like a banshee. But no one is listening to me. Everyone is sleeping peacefully inside their apartments and the car washers are beyond earshot.

I shouldn't lose heart though. I have an unlikely band of allies. The stray dogs that live inside our complex are barking their heads off indignantly, ticked off by the cacophony of mechanical animal sounds. If that doesn't wake the rest of the complex up, I don't know what will. I hope they pee on all the tyres in revenge. I would if I could.

I'm actually rooting for a Grand Theft Auto (GTA) type situation in real life. A situation that involves simultaneous disappearance of the cars with their alarms. Are the car thieves listening?

What is it about people in Gurgaon and their obsession with all things fancy? Including sophisticated car security systems with strobe lights and sirens, no less. From dogs barking to roosters crowing, there isn't a sound that these blasted alarms haven't covered. It's like I'm living in an animal farm.

The one time we had a freak hailstorm in the village, it was almost as though the world had come to an end. Each falling stone set off the wails, siren, strobe lights and mechanical animals. What a spectacle that was. One of those sound and light shows. I can't believe people actually pay money to see that sort of thing!

Do car alarms actually prevent cars from getting stolen? From what I read in the newspapers, car thefts in Gurgaon seem to be on the rise. A couple of cars got stolen in broad daylight from my neighbourhood recently. So the alarms can't really be all that helpful, can they? Apart from nuisance value, they don't seem to have much going for them as far as I can tell. I would love for some of these cars to be nicked. God knows, I need my sleep. But no luck, so far.

I read an article somewhere that said that car alarms are actually quite ineffective. Most of the car-alarm systems that are used in my condominium complex seem to be highly sensitive and they go off multiple times due to the heavy traffic in the zone. And here's the funny thing—the more they go off, the less people pay attention to them.

The article also stated that in cities like New York, citizens have lobbied to get car alarms banned, citing noise pollution and ineffectiveness. Yes, I totally get that. Police departments in the West also recommend other, more effective (and quieter) forms of security, including pager systems alerting the car owner personally if the car is disturbed. Steering-wheel and brake-pedal locks are also some cheaper alternatives that provide better protection against theft. I hear there are less intrusive mobile apps as well.

Are the car alarm owners listening? I doubt it.

Why install something that doesn't actually help keep your car safe? Can everyone wake up please (I've been up since 4 a.m. anyway) and do something about these wretched things? I'm all for security but not at the cost of disturbing others.

Ban? Anyone?

28.

Nightmare on Selfie Street

I was in a Ram Gopal Varma horror flick. Instead of apples, however, people had turned into smartphones, strewn everywhere I looked. I woke up, drenched in sweat, alone in an empty bed. Next to me, in the spot where my husband usually slept, lay an Android phone. In the darkness, I could see a selfie of him flashing on the display screen. I blacked out.

Ever since I went out for dinner to an upscale dining hub in Gurgaon on that fateful evening a couple of days ago, I've been having this recurring nightmare about people turning into phones. You may think I'm headed for a stint in a mental asylum. I can explain and you won't think I'm crazy. Heck, you may even feel my pain.

It was a balmy March evening, spring still in the air. After a particularly tiring week, we had decided to treat ourselves to a hearty Chinese meal at our favourite restaurant.

We should have turned back and sped home the minute we first spotted the serpentine queue of cars waiting to enter the dining hub. That would have been wise. Instead we patiently took our place in the queue and after what seemed like hours, got ushered into a spot by a uniformed attendant. There were people everywhere, thronging towards the entrance, loud music blaring from the loudspeakers, a bizarre mix of pop and trance. Something felt wrong, I couldn't put my finger on it.

It started as soon as we had walked through the security screens. There were people everywhere—young, old, middle-aged, families, couples, schoolgirls, teenagers and children—and wherever I looked, people were taking selfies of themselves, their baes, kitty party groups, families, and kids. They would walk a couple of steps, stop, look around, pout and hold their phones at an angle and click. It was bizarre and a bit scary. We started walking faster, desperate to reach the restaurant and get away from the selfie madness. But it only got worse. There were more people we encountered along the way, more camera phones, more huddles and more selfies.

I could hear voices inside my head:

In shops, in malls,
In front of smelly bathroom stalls,
They're taking selfies everywhere!
With friends and with foes,
Phones held close in front of their nose,
They're taking selfies everywhere!
They stop, they click,
Some as is, while others have a stick,
They're taking selfies everywhere!

The remaining part of the evening is a blur and I'm not sure if I even want to vividly remember. I just remember the people and their phones. The grins, the pouts and the selfies.

'Selfie, Selfie!'

Wait a minute. Who said that? I turn around abruptly.

Are those zombies walking towards me, holding phones at

Nightmare on Selfie Street 99

an abnormal angle to their white faces? Bloodshot eyes, they look like they are going to attack.

I scream. I think I'm having that nightmare again.

Can you blame me?

29.

Turning Japanese

I was at my neighbour's house for dinner. My neighbour, a forty-something housewife from Haryana, had invited a couple of her close friends to celebrate her husband's new job at a Japanese corporation in the Millennium City. She had been talking about it for months. 'I've planned a grand feast for all of you yaar. But please don't make me tell you more, it will ruin the surprise!'

I couldn't help but wonder what the surprise was going to be. I'd been to her house for dinner many times in the past and to be quite honest, the food she served was always the same—black dal with a dollop of cream as garnish, curried cauliflower, paneer masala with peas and raita. The only thing that was different each time was the stuffing inside the piping hot parathas she brought fresh to the dinner table at the start of the meal.

My curiosity was piqued. There weren't a whole lot of vegetables left that she hadn't already stuffed into her parathas. Finally, when the day arrived, I landed up slightly early in front of her house accompanied by my husband and a large bouquet of yellow chrysanthemums. She opened the door after just one ring of the doorbell and ushered us in, all smiles. 'Oh, you shouldn't have bothered with flowers,' she gushed when my husband handed her the flowers. 'These are so pretty,' she said, disappearing into the kitchen to find a vase for them. Within the next half an hour, all the other guests had arrived; her other women friends from the complex with their husbands in tow.

It was time for the big reveal.

She led us into her dining room with a big grin on her face. The table was neatly laid out for the eight of us. There were no plates or dishes or food. Instead, there were eight square plastic cases with chopsticks placed neatly beside them. All around the table, there were small containers filled with colourful sauces. From where I was standing I could make out what the containers had. She had ordered sushi, in celebration of her spouse's new Japanese workplace. That was the surprise.

'Don't worry ji. It's not raw fish,' she giggled when she noticed that several of the ladies around me had turned pale. 'It's tandoori chicken sushi. All cooked shooked. You won't get sick!'

I tried hard to suppress a smile. I noticed my husband was grinning quite openly. He couldn't hide his mirth. But clearly, the woman had managed to surprise everyone, including me. And while the tandoori chicken sushi was delicious, I couldn't help but wonder what the Japanese would think of the desi twist.

I needn't have wondered. It turned out the sushi came from a shop owned by a Japanese couple settled in Gurgaon. 'You must try it,' our hostess exclaimed. 'They have rogan josh flavour also. That would be delicious, no?' The Japanese, it seems, have been selling a lot more than just cars here. I couldn't help but marvel at how perfectly the sushi had been rolled out and adapted to cater to local tastes. It was almost as though tandoori chicken had always been one of the key ingredients of the Japanese dish. The wasabi dip was delicious. While I'm not sure whether the other guests tucked in as heartily as my husband and I did, she had made good on her promise. I had to give her that.

From sushi to bean jam cakes, Teriyaki to Yakimeshi, the

Japanese influence in Gurgaon is hard to miss. There are bakeries turning out Japanese treats while restaurants and sushi outlets are multiplying by the hour. Many local supermarkets have also started stocking Japanese goodies—and one can find sauces, condiments and seaweed boxes among other things.

While the increase in Japanese businesses and corporations in Delhi/NCR have, no doubt, contributed to the sushi invasion, Gurgaon was not giving up its tandoori chicken without a fight. Was the Village turning into a mini-Japan then? Who knows. If the Koreans were already here, could the Japanese be far behind?

From the look of it, they are already here. A couple of days back I saw a group of Japanese tourists being led by a guide around Galleria, a tiny shopping market in my neighbourhood. There were around twelve of them, between the ages of thirty to forty-five. The Indian guide had stopped in front of the Subway store and was telling the group how popular the chain was in Gurgaon. The tourists nodded excitedly, flashing smiles at one another. 'Ah .... Subway,' one of them said. Did I spot one of them take out a camera to click a photograph? Or did I imagine that. I walked on, trying hard to suppress a smile. I'm quite proud of what this place has become.

Yoi Desu, isn't it?

30.

It's a Dog's Life

Did I tell you about Lucky, my neighbour's Saint Bernard puppy? Turns out Lucky wasn't quite lucky after all. His owners, the Chopras, paid a small fortune to buy him from a local dog breeder in Delhi.

'Why don't you get a pug instead?' I had suggested to Mrs Chopra when she announced they were getting a Saint Bernard puppy. The Saint Bernards are large, guard dogs from the western Alps region, not really suitable for Gurgaon's concrete towers and dusty climes.

'To tell you the truth, I don't really want a dog. I'm slightly scared of them,' the woman had confessed, shamefacedly.

'Then, why are you getting one?' I was dumbfounded. I had grown up with five dogs in our Kolkata house, dogs we loved to distraction. One was a Tibetan Apso while the others were mongrels we had adopted from the streets. I couldn't understand why anyone would get a dog if they were scared of them.

'Well, my husband has decided. He wants a dog and that's that. All his friends and colleagues have dogs. Many of our relatives too. Even my Chachu in Sector 5 is getting an Alsatian. So Chopra Sahab is under pressure to get one!' she said sadly, eyes downcast. The Chopras didn't have any children. Having a pet was the next best alternative. They aren't the only family in the Millennium City to feel this kind of pressure.

Canines are prized possessions in Gurgaon. The denizens are very particular about the company they keep, dogs included. Nothing but the very best will do. You will find some of the fanciest breeds in the Village. From Dalmatians, Rottweilers, Retrievers, Labradors, Huskies, Greyhounds, Pekinese, Chihuahuas and others whose names I can't even pronounce.

It's not just the Gucci bags, Emporio Armani suits and the Volkswagen cars, the canines are sourced from the best breeders and pet stores across the country at steep prices and take up pride of place in each household. Most often, the owners are not dog lovers (like the Chopras), merely keeping up with the Joneses; in this case, the Sharmas, Mitras, Yadavs and Chachu from Sector 5.

I thought the Chopras were being ridiculous. Not that I said it out loud to them. If they wanted a pet, they could get a goldfish from the pet store. But a Saint Bernard inside a nine hundred square feet flat? That was a recipe for disaster. I shuddered at the thought. I had grown up in a house full of dogs but we had a huge garden and plenty of space for the dogs to run around and play. I would never consider having a dog in my flat in Gurgaon. At least not a giant like a Saint Bernard.

Turns out they hadn't thought the idea through at all.

Lucky arrived a few months later, a small and cuddly bundle of brown and white fur. I went over to see him. The Chopras were ecstatic, almost as though Mrs Chopra had delivered the puppy from her own womb. They played the doting parents fussing over their new baby. They even hired a new maid to help look after the dog. The girl, Meena, hardly more than a teenager, was tiny with a sullen face. For a while, their lives were perfect.

'Are you sure she knows how to look after a dog?' I asked Mrs Chopra after a few days. 'She doesn't look as though she likes dogs either.' I could see Meena skulking around with an eye on the puppy, who was sleeping peacefully in the middle of the living room.

'Arre, even I don't like dogs. But see how happy I am to get Lucky. He's such a lovely puttar (son). She will also start loving him. How hard can it be?' Mrs Chopra replied genially.

'Is she taking him for walks? Giving him a bath properly, cleaning up when he makes a mess?' I asked anxiously. I couldn't believe that the tiny Meena would be able to do everything efficiently by herself.

'Of course, of course. She is doing all that. What is so hard, tell me?' explained Mrs Chopra. 'Dogs are banned in our park downstairs, no? So I've told her to take him to the terrace. If he does his business there, she flings it off the roof!'

'What?' I said horrified. I couldn't believe what she had just said.

'I said, when he does the big job, she flings it off the roof. Isn't that what people do here?' Mrs Chopra asked innocently.

'No! They most certainly do not!' I screamed out vehemently. 'Where on earth did you get such a preposterous idea?'

'Arre, why are you getting agitated?' she said calmly. 'Mr Chopra read something like this in the papers the other day. About someone who was flinging dog potty from the roof of a condo somewhere in Gurgaon. So he thought, what a good idea. Why not tell our maid to do it too? No jhamela. Just take Lucky to the terrace, get him to do the job and then throw it out. That's what she's been doing.'

I was speechless. When I got my voice back, I explained that it was illegal to throw poop off the rooftop. The maid her husband had read about in the paper was punished because she did it. Her eyes widened as I was telling her the story. 'You need to train her to take him downstairs, onto the main road and clean up after he does his business. People are very fussy here about that sort of thing. You will get into trouble if any one of the residents complain.'

She nodded her head. On my way out, I told Meena in Bengali (yes, she's also from West Bengal, what did you think?) that she shouldn't throw anything from the rooftop. She stared at me sullenly.

Well, they didn't get into any trouble with the other residents, thank heavens. But they weren't able to keep Lucky in the house for much longer either.

Puppies, like human babies, don't stay small forever. They grow. Lucky grew too, into the giant guard dog that he was supposed to be. Soon, he had become too big to be kept in the house. Meena ran away. 'He will eat me up,' were her last words as she ran out of the house one day.

'What do we do? He's become an enormous giant!' Mrs Chopra had shrieked. 'We didn't know he would grow this big. The breeder didn't tell us.' Clearly the latter had left out some important facts about the dog. The Chopras hadn't done their homework either.

Poor Lucky was miserable. He hardly had any room to breathe inside the cramped flat. There was no one to take him out for walks or look after him. Most of the domestic help who doubled up as dog walkers in the complex were scared to come near him. Mr Chopra would be at work the whole day and Mrs Chopra couldn't handle the dog all by herself. So, with a heavy heart, the Chopras had to give Lucky up for adoption. But I hear he went to a loving home and there's plenty of room for him to run around and play.

As for the Chopras, their dog-parenting days are clearly over. Thank God for small mercies. Maybe now they will consider getting a goldfish after all!

31.

Outside the Box

The lady at the other end of the phone line was insistent. 'But I need to know,' she whined, 'are you going to accompany your daughter to the birthday party or is it your maid?' I sighed. I mean, what bloody difference did it make whether it was me or my maid? She just needed to add an extra person to the headcount. Unless she was planning on personalized return gifts for the parents! 'I really can't say at this point,' I growled. 'But it will be an adult for sure. I don't ever leave my daughter unsupervised.' She hung up. I went back to my work, having made up my mind that the little one (she was around five then) would not be attending that party, with or without an adult!

Many months later, I finally found out the real reason behind the daft question. As it happens, it wasn't quite so daft after all. In fact, it was ingenuity of the kind that makes my blood boil. Turns out that maids in this part of the world are not allowed to eat food from the party table. Customized boxes are designed for them. Ones that are handed to them when they leave, to eat in the privacy of their homes or rooms (if they are live-in maids). Thank god for the privacy at least. The stuff that is put in these boxes, I would be ashamed to look at, leave alone eat. Scraps of food. A far cry from the banquet that is laid out at the party for the children and their parents.

Writing this makes my skin crawl, reminding me of that horrid lady and her whiny voice. The same lady I bump into, flashing her diamonds and her chauffeur-driven Mercedes, when I'm on my way to school. 'Cheapskate,' I think to myself while flashing her my brilliant smile. 'You can buy diamonds but can't afford to show your help a good time.'

Over the years, I have had the misfortune of attending some of these parties. Children with an assortment of nannies running after them while they play. Some of these so-called nannies are children themselves, barely twelve or thirteen years old. They are hired to keep an eye on the children and make sure they don't hurt themselves or get into trouble. When food is served from a lavish banquet table laid out with fancy eats, the nannies make sure the kids eat everything on their plates. There's chicken and vegetable burgers, French fries, pasta, chicken nuggets, cheese balls, noodles and birthday cake.

It irks me that the nannies are not allowed to eat at the parties. I can do without the cake and the chicken burger and I won't eat at a party where little girls, probably the same age as my daughter, are fetching and carrying, all the while surreptitiously eyeing the food on the table. They need the food much more than me or my kid.

A dear friend of mine often tries to pacify me when I get worked up. 'There's a reason people have boxes for maids,' she says. 'Who's going to watch the kids when they eat at the party? It is easier if the help just goes home and eat.' Nope. That logic doesn't work for me at all. Don't send the maids to birthday parties then. If you don't want your kids to run amok while the help eats, come and watch them yourself. It might help you lose a calorie or two. Also, this doesn't explain why people put different food in the boxes from what they serve at the party. Inferior, cheap stuff mostly—samosa, a stale sandwich, a dubious-looking sweet.

I know overseas vacations are costly. But does one really need to save money this way?

I run into families dining at fancy restaurants. The entire group sits around the table, stuffing their faces with food from the plates in front of them. The maid sits in a chair at the far end, usually minding the babies and small children, looking extremely awkward the whole time. No food is ever served to her.

I bumped into an Arab family in Starbucks recently. Dad, burkha-clad mother, little girl and baby in a pram with a nanny following closely on their heels. The whole family pigged out on coffee, croissants, carrot cake and cookies while the nanny sat in the corner, patting the inconsolable baby (who probably wanted milk) and no one offered a morsel of food to her!

I wish, for once in their lives, these people would think outside the box. They might have to forgo that skiing vacation. But in the end, they would die happy.

32.

Driving Miss Daisy

Perhaps it's just as well that I can't and don't drive a car in the Village. Can you imagine the increase in the number of road rage incidents if I did?

Over the years, I've encountered a 'significant' (why be polite, let's change that to 'phenomenal') number of bad drivers in Gurgaon. Most of them, unfortunately, have been women!

No, I'm not sorry I said that. So don't look all hurt and distressed and cluck your tongue at me. I may be a woman but that is no reason to be biased.

Most of my women friends drive their own cars and there are a handful of them I would trust with my life. The rest of them? Well, let's just say I politely decline their offers of giving me a ride every time. Thank you very much for your offer but I love my life too much to give it up so soon.

'According to the American Automobile Association, men may be responsible for more accidents than women, but the gap is getting smaller. Today, more women drive (and drive more) than ever before, which has the unfortunate consequence of an increase in speeding, aggressive driving and even fatal crashes among women.' (*Readers Digest*)

Also, given what happened this morning, I have a right to be upset.

I was returning home from running errands, weighed down by several grocery bags. There is a tiny lane that I have to cross to get home from the market next door. So there I was, crossing the lane slowly (after having looked in both directions) when, all of a sudden, she came out of nowhere. Like a bat out of hell. I stepped back onto the pavement in alarm, dropping a few of my bags in the process. To top it all, the woman had the gall to give me a dirty look as she whizzed past after having been the one at fault.

Now I don't have any gall to call my own. My poor, infected gall bladder was removed two years back. But I do have plenty of gaalis. So I yelled at the speeding car once I had regained my composure and grabbed my bags.

'Imbecile!' 'Nincompoop!' 'Dumbass!' 'Stupid Cow!'

Now don't get me wrong. I'm not normally a bad-tempered person. But don't expect me to be pleasant if you are trying to kill me first thing in the morning and are not in the least bit remorseful about it. Bad driving I can still tolerate but recklessness and aggression completely puts me off.

A few days ago, on my way to pick up my daughter from school, I witnessed another accident. It happened right in front of me. A woman rammed into an autorickshaw while trying to park her car. Instead of being apologetic, she decided to get all high and mighty and make a great show of her aggression. She stormed out of her car, a tiny little thing, yanked the key out of the auto's ignition, made a few calls and started yelling at him as though the entire episode was his fault. 'Do you know who I am? Do you know who I am?' she kept saying, like a stuck record. Obviously the poor man had no clue. He just wanted his keys back. But the lady refused to hand them over. She marched into her car and drove off with his keys!

I agree that auto drivers in the Village are a menace but you don't bully people without just cause. Driving a fancy car does not give you the right to get away with wrongdoing! At least not as far as I'm concerned.

It makes me fume to even think about it.

I wonder where all these ladies get their driving licences from. If they own one, that is. I remember my neighbour telling me that she could get me a licence if I wanted to start driving. 'You should get a licence, it is really necessary ji!'

Get a licence? What about learning to drive first? Having been brought up in a city where one was usually driven around by chauffeurs, I didn't really get much of an opportunity to learn. Not that I ever had any inclination. I was lazy as hell.

It's different here. Most people drive their own cars. Men and women. And that should be a good thing, in practice.

Except for the fact that things don't exactly happen in the right order here. So you can pay and get a licence and then learn to drive. That must be what happened with the lady who backed her car onto my foot (almost) without looking in the rear-view mirror or honking the other day. How could she be at fault? She must have gotten a licence and then learned to drive! Or not!

I must clarify, however, that not all women drivers in the NCR drive badly. There are a few, who I can safely take a ride with, without fearing for my life. A handful of girls who drive skillfully, zipping their vehicles this way and that, as they negotiate the twists and turns of this unpredictable place. These are people I trust with my life. Literally speaking or I wouldn't get into their car otherwise! Thank god for these women, you know who you are. I've told you often enough.

As for the others? God bless them and keep them far away from me.

33.

Buzz

Wasps hate me with a vengeance.

Ever since I sat on one (mistakenly, of course) and sent it to its squashy, painful death some sixteen years and twenty-two pounds ago, the entire species seems to have targeted me for annihilation by stinging.

Let me tell you how it all happened.

I had walked into my flat one evening after work. Power outages were frequent in our neighbourhood those days and our condominium had been without power the whole day. The entire flat was pitch-dark save for one corner of the living room that was illuminated by the moonlight streaming in from the large glass windows next to the dining table. I headed towards the wrought iron dining table, drew a chair out and flopped down on it clumsily, hoping to sit it out till the power was restored. My husband was groping around in the kitchen trying to make himself a cup of tea.

No sooner had I sat down, I felt a sharp prick on the back of my thigh through my cotton trousers. Thinking it was a rubber band from the cardboard egg carton that I had unpacked that morning, I reached for the spot and rubbed it. Instantly the prick had become a burning ache, radiating to the rest of my leg. Alarmed, not sure of what was happening, I shouted out for my husband. The flame from his cigarette lighter revealed a tiny wasp lying dead as a doorknob on the cushion underneath me, flattened by the weight of my body. Meanwhile, the pain had gotten worse and my thigh had swollen up like a sausage.

An anti-allergic tablet and some slaked lime from the paanwala who sat across the road from our house made the pain and swelling go away in the next few hours. But I had learnt a lesson I was not likely to forget in a hurry.

Never again would I sit on any surface in Gurgaon without investigating it thoroughly first!

I'm not sure what the poor dead wasp would have learnt but its enraged brethren had marked me for death. I was a marked woman. I was Liam Neeson of *Taken 2*.

The worst part was that there was nowhere left to hide. Come warm weather and Gurgaon was suddenly swarming with wasps, with wasp colonies taking up residence in every damn place! Unlike other insects, wasps nest all over the place, not just in trees and shrubs. Holes in the ground, spaces under homes, wall cavities, lofts.

My block of flats, for instance, is a popular nesting ground. In fact, come to think of it, wherever I've lived (in the last nineteen years) in Gurgaon, wasps have coexisted in dangerously close proximity. Some might refer to it as a strange twist of fate.

At least, I'm not allergic to stings, from wasps and other bugs. Thank the Lord for small mercies. Not that it helps.

I was out shopping for groceries the other day when one of them attacked me. Flying menacingly near my face, the sneaky bug tried stinging me twice. Both times I swung my shopping bag wildly at it before running for cover inside the guard post near the gate. A group of maids watching the show shouted out at me to hide my shocking yellow Lumia cell phone, 'Didi, it's coming to you because of the phone!' What a tech-savvy creature, I thought as I ran for my life, flinging the phone inside the bag I was carrying.

I had changed the phone that same evening, choosing a dull black one instead.

A couple of days later, I got a call from my daughter's school. Turns out a wasp colony had taken up residence outside her classroom and the wasps had started getting into the classrooms and bothering the teachers and students. So they had decided to send the kids home and fumigate the nest with kerosene!

I've often fantasized about having a superhuman alter-ego. Boring, frumpy housewife in the daytime, fighting crime by night dressed in one of those sexy leather suits, ridding the Village of all its vices. Even Liam Neeson wasn't ready to be put down without a fight. Perhaps my encounter with wasps can be put to some good use? All I need is a radioactive wasp to sting me and I can morph into Wasp Aunty!

Are you laughing at me? Well, hold on for a second there. Wasp Aunty would have some serious mutant powers. How else would I fit into a leather suit? And if Batman can make such a cool superhero with his fear of bats, why not your friendly neighbourhood Wasp Aunty?

I may not be particularly friendly or neighbourly in person but it's my alter-ego we are talking about. She would be everything I'm not. And her sting would be worse than her bite. So, get your repellants ready.

Buzzzz!

34.
Beauty and the Beastly

The Hulk was stirring next to me.

I cast an uneasy glance towards where he sat, sprawled back in a leather recliner, hands hanging over the sides of the seat. The green goop on his face was trickling down his neck and his mouth was slightly open. Everywhere I looked, there was an abundance of brawn. It wasn't a pretty sight. But then again, I wasn't Betty Ross. Far from it, in fact.

I was just an ordinary woman who had walked into a Gurgaon salon on a Sunday afternoon for her ritual monthly shearing. I was hoping that the place would be empty other than a few pretty young things getting themselves beautified for their weekend parties. Imagine my surprise, horror rather, when I found the place crawling with men of various shapes and sizes, getting their hair, faces and even nails groomed.

Before I could run out of the place, my hairdresser had spotted me, accosted me and pushed me towards a chair near the reception area. 'Pliz take a seat madam, I'll be done soon. It's wedding season na, that's why the rush.' Throwing me an apologetic look, he hurried back to the elderly man he had been tending to. I could hear the *whirr* of the blow-dryer as he went back to his business of drying man-locks carefully. Sheesh. I looked away.

I heard someone grunt next to me. The Hulk had woken up, and was sitting up in his chair, staring at me. I didn't know whether to laugh or scream in terror. A diminutive salon attendant rushed to his side and started wiping the green goop off his face with cotton wool. 'Your face will be much fresher after this treatment sir, all the blackheads will also be gone,' the little man was telling the Hulk in Hindi. The Hulk merely grunted and stared at his reflection in the mirror, waiting for all the goop to come off and a fresh new face to emerge.

I stared at that reflection, half expecting Eric Bana or Edward Norton to stare back at me once the green stuff was wiped off. Or if I was really lucky, Mark Ruffalo. No such luck. If you asked me, the bloke looked nicer with the green muck on his face. I was getting angsty now.

Behind where I was sitting, two loud gents, Lucky and Honey, were getting their beards tended and hands massaged. They sounded as though they were arguing with one another but it was a friendly conversation really. That's how people have a friendly conversation in Haryana, I've learnt. One of them, I gathered, was getting married and the other (probably his brother) was telling him that he would be buying several Diesel jackets for him as his trousseau. No, money didn't seem to be an issue. The one getting his hands massaged had an abundance of rings on his fingers, like our own Bappi da. Midway through the hand massage, a tall uniformed chauffeur strolled in and handed Honey a fat wallet. He had left it in the BMW. Honey was all chuckles and waved the driver off.

I didn't want them to think I was staring at them, which I was, so I looked away. From mud masks to henna, there were men around me in various stages of beautification that I wish to god I hadn't witnessed. Enough to give me nightmares for days! Other than me, there wasn't a woman in sight.

The newspapers have been writing about Delhi's famous wedding season—in fact, one of the days last year saw 25,000 weddings! Can you believe that? Little wonder that all these men were queuing up to look gorgeous.

Who said that vanity was a woman's preserve? Not a man from Gurgaon for sure!

35.

Santa Claus Is Coming to Town

Santa's coming!
Yeah yeah yeah yeaoooh
Santa Claus is coming to town

I'm really wishing now that he wasn't.

A lady has been belting out Christmas carols over a microphone at the school next door the whole morning. She has a raucous voice and is completely out of tune. I've never heard such a dreadful rendition of *Rudolph the Raad Nosed Reindeer* in my life! Now she's murdering *Santa Claus is Coming to Town*. I wonder how long this torture is going to continue. I'm tempted to try the Ice Bucket Challenge on her. That ought to shut her up. Dampen her enthusiasm perhaps?

You might think I'm like the Grinch who stole Christmas. Whoville, however, is nothing like Gurgaon. There's absolutely nothing to steal here. Other than my friendly neighbourhood carol singer's dreadful voice! She's a menace to society.

Christmas is just not Christmas in Gurgaon. Other than the bright green faux Made-in-China Christmas trees that I find at the market next door and the overpriced plum cakes in all the local bakeries, there is nothing here that remotely resembles the Yuletide spirit that I've grown up in. The shopkeeper at one of the shops nearby has been trying to sell me a battery-operated doorbell that goes 'Jingle Jingle' in a bhangra tune every time someone presses it. 'It's the latest thing madam!' he says excitedly, waving the offensive thing in front of my eyes. 'Everyone is buying it for Christmas. You must buy one for your house!'

I've been living far away from home for many, many years so you would think I'd be quite used to it by now. Detached. Impassionate. Isn't that what this place does to you? Yet each year feels the same. That longing to walk down familiar lanes, jostle with crowds to buy Christmas trees, baubles and confectionery, aroma of freshly baked cakes in the air.

There isn't a single market here that can hold a candle to the Christmas markets back home in Kolkata. The swanky malls don't count. They don't have the right ambience, even though one of them is called Ambience! There's none of that familiar excitement or buzz in the air. The Christmas bazaars at the foreign missions are just too…foreign! There's everything on display (from stoles to German sausages), yet you don't find what you're looking for.

The trek to the market for buying Christmas baubles for the tree, the familiar dingy stalls with the bottlebrush trees, crackers and decorations spilling out, the sausage rolls and rum balls from the tea room at Flurys, the aroma of Christmas cake and kulkuls, the smiling faces behind the counter, the midnight mass at St Thomas Church, the customary walk down Park Street on Christmas day, the Christmas brunches and lunches hosted by friends and relatives at the different clubs of Kolkata.

Gurgaon has none of that. The newspapers are full of advertisements. Hotels advertising exorbitantly-priced Christmas brunches, lunches and parties graced by some Bollywood celebrity or the other. I never feel like going to any of them. We have an oversized shiny green bottlebrush in our living room which I decorate with knick-knacks from my collection. I bake a cake, listen to some Christmas music and that's it.

I'm kind of relieved when all of it is over each year. Don't get me wrong. I know 'tis the season to be jolly and all that. But as you can see, it's really hard to be jolly in Gurgaon during Christmas.

Also, once the festivities are over, I can safely step outside and not have to run into a creepy-looking Santa at a local mall or shopping complex. And no, it's not about my daughter. I'm the one who's scared of the emaciated red-suited figures with masks that could be horror movie props. That fixed grin and the eyes that move behind the slits give me the shudders, I tell you.

Christmas at the Village is all about the creepy Santas! Even the Grinch would be a welcome sight next to them.

Is there a shortage of overweight, elderly men with white hair willing to take on the job in our country? Do the brands, companies, malls or multiplexes even realize just how terrified most children are when they come face-to-face with these characters? Santa often has Charlie Chaplin and Batman's Joker as his unlikely sidekicks. Charlie's face is deathly white and the Joker isn't remotely joker-ish. The common feature is that they are all poker thin. They look like they haven't eaten in days, maybe months. A few pillows as padding wouldn't have hurt, boys. They may have helped prevent all the tears and the confusion. Santa in a storybook and Santa in real life. Oh my god, what happened?

Many years ago, we were invited to a Christmas party organized by a company I used to work for. It was an elaborate affair at a farmhouse in Gurgaon. There were stalls with different kinds of food, goody bags, activities and games for the kids. And Santas. Zillions of them, all over the place, tugging along sacks of chocolates which they would hand out to the kids. Each time my daughter ran into one, she would turn white, freeze and burst into tears. The Santa, in question, not sure what his problem was, would keep hounding her with chocolates. And she would bawl her heart out, running this way and that. He would follow, running after her. Can you imagine her predicament? She was just two then and Santa(s) had scared the living daylights out of her!

She's much older now. She eyes them warily and maintains a safe distance whenever she spots them at a mall or a cinema hall. In fact, she alerts me when there's one within our zone. We escape into a store or a café till the coast is clear. I have many friends who avoid shopping during this time as their babies are scared of the local St Nicks'. I have a hunch it's not just their babies.

Someone has just asked the carol singer next door for an encore. Are people hard of hearing? She started again, *You better watch out—Santa Claus is comiiiing to town. Yeah yeah yeah yeaoooh!*

Give me some arsenic. Make it quick.

36.

Mind Your Language

My neighbourhood clinic has put up a notice that says 'We have shifted to the backside.' What a ridiculous thing to write on an official noticeboard! Whose backside are they talking about? When I asked the shopkeeper at the store next door where the clinic had moved to, he explained that they had relocated to a temporary office at the rear end of the complex. Now officially known as the backside.

Granted that writing comprehensible English is not everyone's forte. It's not even our mother tongue. Why write it then? Why not put up a notice in Hindi that would explain where their new whereabouts were?

It's not our language and we are not expected to be fluent. You can't fault us for trying though, can you? You could admire our confidence as we make one blunder after another, often causing situations of undeniable hilarity or distress.

I went for a mandatory annual health checkup at a leading hospital in the Village recently. After I had paid the bill for the tests, the nurse told me, 'Madam, can you please come to our backside? We will do the tests there.'

I couldn't stop giggling helplessly causing all the other people gathered at the reception to glance suspiciously at me. I couldn't help it. Go to the backside for a test. Why on earth would I go to your, or anyone else's backside for a test! It looked as though Gurgaon's medical fraternity were taken with their backsides.

My neighbour Mrs Chopra called me the other day. She had invited some of her friends for tea and was wondering whether I would like to join them.

'Where?' I asked her. I didn't know whether she was entertaining at home or at her favourite café at the neighbourhood market.

'Where Hair,' she replied cheerfully.

'Excuse me?' I wondered whether I had heard right.

'Where Hair,' she repeated slowly.

I couldn't understand why she was asking about my hair all of a sudden. My hair was on my head. I touched it all the same to make sure. It was piled up untidily in a bun on top of my scalp.

'My hair is on my head, Mrs Chopra,' I said coldly. 'Why do you ask? Where else would it be?'

'Arre yaar. I'm not talking about your hair. I said we are *hair*, in my place only! Come over.'

I realized that she was asking me to go over to her place. That's where her friends had gathered!

It wasn't my hair after all. It was *here*. But it was a hair-raising experience all the same.

Reminds me of another hysterical incident that happened many years ago, when I had moved to Gurgaon. One evening after work, a few of us were discussing the office fancy dress party and what we were planning to wear. Our discussion might have been a bit too animated for we soon saw our young, Canadian boss peering at us rather curiously from the door which connected our offices to his. One of my colleagues, a pretty twenty-something, who I always suspected of being soft on the boss, yelled out to him, 'Come on over, join us. We were talking about our costumes for the party next week.' He smiled and walked across, looking bemused. 'Yeah, that thing next week. I was wondering what to go as myself.' My colleague shouted, 'You could go as Full Monty. That's your national costume isn't it?'

As the rest of us gaped at her in horror not wanting to see the boss's white face turn beetroot red, I realized that she was not aware of the turmoil she had caused with her naïve outburst. She stared at the boss quizzically wondering why he had turned crimson and wouldn't meet her eye. I realized then that she had confused the Canadian Mounted Police (which was the country's national police force) with *The Full Monty*, a British movie about male strippers. She wasn't asking him to turn up buck naked at the party. Much as she liked him, she wasn't being forward. She just didn't know the language well enough to understand or appreciate that there was a difference.

Thankfully for the young chap, he soon got transferred back to his home country and has hopefully been able to dismiss this unfortunate incident from his mind. I haven't! On a day, when I am feeling particularly low, I think about the expression on his face and it's like an instant mood-lifter. It does give me a few giggles.

Then there was this other time, when the academic dean of a top university in UK was interviewing prospective applicants for a Master's degree course in engineering. The young student in front of her was confident, a bit too confident I thought. When asked about the year he graduated, he said 'Madam, I passed out in 2000.' The British lady looked concerned. 'You passed out? Why? Were you unwell?'

Another student cheerfully whispered to me, after the same session, 'Madam, I will knock you at 10.00 a.m. tomorrow!' As I glared at him, unable to speak for a moment, he continued in the same airy fashion, 'I will give you a knock, if you are in office, I will come in and talk to you.' No, he wasn't making an indecent proposal. He was just telling me he would knock on my door. Thank God for that.

I could go on. There are so many anecdotes, funny yet tragic in a sense. Like a colleague at a party who told me that I was vertile. I stared at him for several minutes. Vertile? What on earth was that? Was he suggesting that I was virile or fertile? Why on earth would he suggest either? On what basis? Thankfully, the drift of the conversation soon made me realize that he meant to say that I was versatile. And no, he wasn't drunk. He thought vertile was a word in the English language.

What can I say? We are like this only.

37.

Sex and the City

There's no way Vyasa, the writer of the epic narrative *Mahabharata*, could have known that his work would come in handy in teaching kids in Gurgaon schools about the birds and the bees.

'Do you know how Guru Dronacharya was born?' my daughter asked me the other day in between giggles.

I groaned. I had a feeling that I wouldn't like the answer very much.

She is studying the epic in school. Though lately, I've been wishing she wasn't. It's not that I am against children learning about ancient Hindu mythology and culture. It's the questions afterwards that I am not prepared for. Questions that have nothing to do with History but Biology, in fact.

She paced the room with her textbook in her hands giggling, observing me all the while. 'His father, Rishi Bharadwaja saw a gorgeous apsara and got turned on,' she snorted. 'He produced a reproductive fluid which he collected in a vessel, known as a drona, and Dronacharya immediately sprang to life from the vessel. Ta da!' The last bit was announced dramatically, with a flourish.

'Tell me, is it even possible?' she came close, the pupils of her eyes enlarged, incredulous. Her voice was hardly a whisper now.

'What is possible?' I asked blandly.

'Making babies that way?

I gulped. There was silence for a heart-stopping instant as I wracked my brains for a suitable answer.

Finally, it came to me. 'Why not? Haven't you heard about test tube babies? Perhaps, this was when the concept started! A drona or a vessel instead of a test tube.'

She looked slightly puzzled. 'But he would need some of the women's stuff too Mama. He can't produce a baby all by himself!'

She did have a point. But what was I to do? I wasn't there when it happened and Vyasa is hardly a reliable source while explaining Biology.

A few days ago, there was another commotion in their class. One of the boys went up to the teacher in front of the entire class and enquired politely how Dhritarashtra had produced 100 children. The fellow, in question, was one of the naughtiest boys in the grade. 'How did a blind man copulate a hundred times Ma'am and that too, with the same woman?' he asked cheerfully, adding, 'I'm sure his wife was cheating on him Ma'am.'

The horrified teacher had marched him to the principal's office. I'm really not sure what I would have done in her place.

Children these days seem to be a lot more aware about things than we were as kids. Is it the Gurgaon effect or something to do with the way we are raising them, I wonder?

I remember the time, several years ago when she had asked me what a prostitute was. Regaining my composure suitably (in time), I had tried to answer her question as best as I could. When she said, 'Oh I see,' and walked away with a toss of her curly head, I realized that my palms were sweaty and my heart was beating very fast. She hadn't noticed, of course.

In a country where we get all tongue-tied and shy talking about the thing that must not be talked about, you might find my behaviour very odd indeed.

But then again, I'm not what you might call a 'normal' parent.

Walk into my home any evening and you might find me and my tween propped up in bed watching the latest episode of *The Secret Life of an American Teenager* and having a heated discussion on how having babies when you are in high school is not a great idea. 'That is so not cool dude,' the twelve-year-old would be saying, mouth twisted derisively while I would reprimand her for the millionth time with 'I am not a dude!'

Hardly something a model Indian parent would do, right?

Wrong.

I have always believed that the best thing any parent (Indian or otherwise) can possibly do for his or her child is to keep the lines of communication open. I've seen my mother doing it (with hilarious consequences) and now it's my turn. Talk, talk, talk. About everything under the sun. Good, bad and the ugly.

In an age where kids can get (mis)information from almost anywhere, I'd prefer that she got the right information from me. At home, or at school from her teachers. Or the…erm… *Mahabharata*?

I don't want to shy away from talking about the birds and the bees and risk my daughter finding out when it's too late. I want to be able to put the information out there and help her make the right choices. Watching *The Big Bang Theory* on the telly may not necessarily be the best way to help her learn but I am not looking for an award for parenting. One-size-fits-all does not work here.

Sex is not a bad word. At least, not in our home. Although, it wasn't always like this.

I still remember my daughter storming into my bedroom when she was five, accusation writ large on her baby face. 'Mama, why did you tell me that babies come from a mama's tummy? That the doctor had taken me out of your tummy?' Oh, the look of disdain on her face. I also remember breaking out in cold sweat, fingers paralyzed on my keyboard, dreading what she would say next.

As it turned out, a little boy in her class who had an older brother had 'helpfully' volunteered with the information about natural childbirth. The process of sex education had begun. Though not quite in the manner I had expected.

Since then, the questions haven't stopped. In fact, I encourage them. Throw them at me, I say. On a good day, I'll answer everything. On a bad day, I'll bark at her and tell her to ask me later. And she always does. There's no escaping that child.

Tween: Why do they have "sex" on my ID card Mama? It's a bad word isn't it?

Me: 'Sex' isn't a bad word, it indicates (on your ID card) whether you are a boy or a girl.

Tween (rolling her eyes provocatively): Of course, 'sex' is a bad word!

Me (slightly exasperated): What do you think 'sex' means?

Tween (coyly): You know, kissing and stuff.

Me (really exasperated): Ok smartass, then what should your ID card say instead of 'sex'?

Tween: Easy! Gender.

I think it's always a good idea to talk to your children. Now is as good a time as any. They may end up teaching you a thing or two. I know mine did. Okay, some of it came from our epics as well. I've now learnt that a man can produce a child inside a cup without a woman's help.

I wonder what the warrior mystic would have to say about that.

38.

Doctor Doctor

Turns out that German philosopher Friedrich Nietzsche was right. What doesn't kill you makes you stronger. Wait, that wasn't Nietzche, that was Kelly Clarkson, the pop singer. I think Nietzsche said, 'That which does not kill us, makes us stronger.'

I have a strong hunch he may have been talking about some Gurgaon doctors.

When the doctor told me that I was pregnant a couple of years ago, I didn't realize that instead of delivering a gurgling, wailing bundle of joy, I would be delivering a rotten gall bladder instead.

Intrigued? Let me tell you all about it.

On the wrong side of forty, I was hardly elated when the doctor confirmed the (good) news at her office about a baby being on its way and all. Not that I needed her to tell me. I had made the discovery myself thanks to the pregnancy kit I had bought from the market. This wasn't my first pregnancy. I just wanted her to tell me that I was wrong, and that the nausea that I felt each morning wasn't really morning sickness but indigestion from stuffing my face with far too many Pepitos from the French bakery next door.

She didn't. It wasn't.

'You don't look happy,' she said, peering at me through her

black-rimmed spectacles, after she had delivered the news. I was sitting there, brows knitted in a frown, not the usual ecstatic mom-to-be. Being delivered the 'good news' is an event of epic proportions in North India. I've had so many people ask me over the years whether I had any 'good news' to share or not. Before I had my first baby that is. My extended family, my siblings, the nosy lady at the tailoring boutique. Even the old grandma who came to sit beside me at the park sometimes.

I shook my head and told the doctor that no, I wasn't exactly over the moon. I wasn't young, had a host of medical problems and didn't want to upset the apple cart with a new baby. I had a job, my first-born had just turned ten and I just didn't want to go through the whole baby routine again. Please, could I abort?

'Nonsense,' I remember her saying. 'Plenty of people have kids at this age. There's nothing to worry about. Your daughter will be thrilled! No question of an abortion.'

She was right about the daughter being thrilled. 'I knew it!' the ten-year-old screamed excitedly when I told her the news that afternoon. 'I saw that… ahem… preggy kit… in the bathroom the other day.' Good Lord, kids these days! They know everything. Yet I couldn't help but smile at her enthusiasm. Perhaps the doctor was right. It wasn't that big a deal.

So, I got myself used to the idea of having a baby in the house in another nine months' time.

Having a baby on the wrong side of forty is not uncommon. Plenty of women have babies when they are older. What the doctor had completely forgotten to tell me, however, was that pregnancies after 40 years of age were generally considered high-risk and older women needed to be careful. Careful meant not lugging heavy stuff (read: grocery bags) or moving things (read: rearranging furniture on a whim). All she had said cheerily was 'continue with your normal life. All is well.'

So I did continue with my normal life and lost the baby in a month's time.

The funny thing was, while I had not been elated to welcome the little thing into the world, I felt a little empty inside, when I lost her. Or maybe it was a him. I would never know. My daughter would never have a sibling. Stray thoughts such as these crowded my mind as I sat there woodenly in the radiologist's office after she had told me the news after a routine USG. 'What should I do next?' I wondered out aloud. 'I have no idea,' the radiologist told me, rather cruelly if I may add. 'You need to call your husband and discuss it with him. How would I know what you should do?'

Perhaps, be more sympathetic? That might help, you silly woman.

I cursed her under my breath and headed straight to the doctor's office. I had a bone to pick with her.

I needn't have bothered. She looked at me with disinterest and said, 'I'm sorry but you should have done your homework.' Her body language said 'I couldn't care less. You aren't a client anymore. So scram!'

Before I left, she told me that I needed to induce a medical miscarriage since it hadn't happened on its own and wrote out names of drugs I needed to make that happen. But the worst wasn't over. The drugs she prescribed led to a severe haemorrhage. I nearly bled to death for the next few months. When I was up and running again, I soon discovered that the drugs from the induced labour had an adverse impact on my gall bladder which shrivelled and died over the next couple of months and I had to have an emergency surgery towards the end of the year.

That is how my second born turned out to be a dead gallbladder. The gall of it, one would think.

Still, at least I am alive to tell the tale.

39.
The Ladies of Gurugram

The other day, I overheard two mothers having a heated discussion outside my daughter's school.

'My daughter is really confused about what she should study after her Class XII examination. I don't know what I should advise her,' one of them was saying.

'Babes, I have the same problem,' shrieked the other excitedly. 'We have to help them make the right decision. But what to tell them?'

The two women stared at each other for several seconds.

Then Mummy #1 had a brainwave. 'I know I don't want her to study law. That is something I am sure about.' She said.

'But why? Law is a good subject, no?' Mummy #2 looked puzzled.

'Arre, have you seen a single female lawyer who is happily married?' Mummy #1 explained, giggling. 'They are either divorced or single. Frankly speaking, I'm not surprised. They are supposed to put in long hours at work, even work over weekends. Which man would put up with that kind of work schedule, you tell me?' she clucked her teeth. 'I know my husband wouldn't. I have to be home when he comes back from work. Have hot rotis and sabzi ready. Nahi, definitely not law babes. She may end up very rich and successful but what good is that without a husband and babies?'

Mummy #2 nodded, eyes widening as realization slowly dawned. 'You are right. We have to make these girls choose something that won't stand in the way of them having happy marriages! Career is good but it can't be too demanding! Something on the side maybe.'

I walked away unable to believe what I was hearing. Having a career on the side? Could you have a career on the side? You could have an order of French fries on the side. A garden salad or even a soft drink perhaps. But a career?

I turned back to take one last look at them before I got into my car. Mummy #1 was wearing a purple velour tracksuit, designer sunglasses shading her eyes, hair in a ponytail, a Coach crossbody bag across her torso. Mummy #2 was wearing a pale blue sweater and fitting denims, coiffured hair, Louis Vuitton bag on her wrist. It was a weekday morning and they didn't look as though they were headed to office. In fact neither of them looked as though they had worked a single day in their lives. Their husbands probably worked in multinational corporations or in real estate.

Wonder what Indra Nooyi would have said to them. Or the happily married female lawyers these women didn't have the good fortune of knowing. These women didn't think women could have it all. I felt sad for their daughters whose futures they were in the process of wrecking with their well-meaning but ill-researched advice.

On second thoughts, I don't feel sorry for their daughters. If they are the sort of girls who bully others for eating sausage buns during the Navratri, I'm not sorry for them at all. They can grow up and have careers on the side while they have hot rotis and fresh sabzi ready for their husbands in the evening and fast for their well-being on festival days.

Like the woman at my daughter's Kumon class. I see her twice a week as she sits in the corner of the brightly-lit reception area poring into an iPhone checking her WhatsApp messages. After a while, she picks up her gold iPhone 7 and whispers into it, '*Raat ke liye bhindi chop karke rakhna!*' I stare at her amazed. What a waste of an iPhone, I think to myself. The woman smiles at me. 'I'm telling the maid to keep the vegetables chopped and ready for me. I will make dinner when I return.' Not that I asked her but she goes on to tell me that she never relinquishes her hold of the kitchen. Even for a day. 'Even when I travel for work, I always tell my maid what to cook for dinner. If I'm not cooking dinner myself that is. I usually do.' She is the VP of a leading e-commerce firm in the Millennium City. 'I can't ask my husband to manage the kitchen no?' she says.

Why not? I don't say this out loud, of course. But why can't the husband take over the kitchen when the wife is busy? It's not just her home. He also lives there, eats there. Why can't he help from time to time? How can he expect his wife to fly if her wings are tied to the kitchen? Not that this woman seems to mind. Like the Gurgaon mothers I encountered on the road the other day. Looks like her career too is on the side. I wonder whether law was ever an option for her.

Modern, literate women who happily fast for their husbands, smear their foreheads and faces with vermillion and pray for happy marriages. The same women are juggling a career on the side, making presentations or sealing a deal or chugging down mugfuls of beer with their office colleagues at the local pubs. Running back home just in time to roll out the rotis. It's like a puzzle, pieces of which just don't fit for me.

Gurugram women. Stuck somewhere between myth and reality. Much like the Village they inhabit. Outward trappings of fancy yet unbelievably archaic inside.

40.

What's in a Name?

My friends have been raving about a new domestic help agency that has set up shop in our neighbourhood. 'You must try them out,' one of them tells me. 'They are not like any other agency. Their staff is well-mannered, trained and experts in housework and cooking.'

I'm tempted. Ever since my helper, Chaina, went back to her village with her husband, I've been a little out of sorts. I can't help thinking how wonderful it would be to have someone efficient take charge of the house once again. And with that thought in mind, I pull out the visiting card that my friends have left for me and call the Happy Helper agency for an appointment.

The woman they send to my door a week later is a round-faced, genial woman (from West Bengal) who goes by the name Shakti. When I ask her where she has worked before, she says breezily, 'Mongolia, Didi. I was working in a flat in Mongolia.'

I stare at her for several minutes, not sure what I should say next. I'm really impressed that she has worked in Mongolia. An expat maid would be quite the conversation piece. Not to mention the exotic Mongol dishes she must have learnt to cook. That would definitely put Mrs Chopra's tandoori sushi to shame. She's wearing a red printed cotton saree, not very different from the other domestic helpers I see around the place, along with a large bindi and a clumsy splotch of sindoor on her forehead. She doesn't look as though she's lived anywhere other than her village in West Bengal. I wonder how she coped, living in a place as remote as that.

'How did you manage? Were your employers Indian?' I ask her.

She giggles. 'I managed quite well, Didi. Why wouldn't I? It was a flat just like yours. And my employers were Bengalis too. They gave me machh bhath (fish rice) every day. But they had to move so I had to look for another job.'

This was globalization indeed. A Bengali family who lived in Mongolia had recruited a Bengali maid. It was true, the world had become a smaller place!

'So how did you come back from Mongolia? In an airplane?' I asked her. She stared at me, dumbfounded. 'Why would I come in an airplane? I came in a cycle rickshaw!'

And that's when the globalization bubble burst. At least for me. She hadn't worked in Mongolia at all but Magnolias, the upscale condominium down the road.

Magnolias, Aralias, Carlton, Wellington, Palm Drive, Rodeo Avenue—Gurgaon's residences and roads have names that are meant to roll off the tongue. Exotic, *phoren* names. Names meant to reflect Gurgaon's kindred connections with international cities such as Los Angeles, Toronto, London, among others. While Gurgaon has failed to deliver on the promise of being a global city like the others, the names have ended up being worth a lot in terms of entertainment value. Malapropisms abound with hilarious consequences.

A lady stuck her head out of the car the other day when I was waiting at the bus stop for my daughter's school bus to arrive. 'Excuse me,' she said. 'I need to get to Hemanta Court. Do you know where that is?' From the look of it, she had been searching

What's in a Name? 139

for it for quite a while. Exhaustion was written all over her pretty face, beads of sweat covered her brow.

I had no idea where Hemanta Court was located. As much as I find the names of most of Gurgaon's residential colonies ridiculous, this one certainly took the cake. Hemanta Court? That sounded like something straight out of Kolkata. I shook my head apologetically. I told her that I knew of a Hamilton Court nearby but I had never heard of a Hemanta Court!

She smiled, looking relieved. 'Yes, that must be it. Hamilton Court. My driver had written the address down in Hindi and it's quite clear that he made a mistake. I was also wondering why the flat had such as peculiar name.'

We grinned at each other. She waved and the car sped off to Hemanta Court, sorry, Hamilton Court.

Gurgaon's obsession with the *phoren* and fanciful isn't new.

I remember being ecstatic to find a large building near the rented apartment we lived in that went by the name of Edmonton Shopping Mall. We had just moved from Kolkata to Gurgaon and I was rather despondent to find that there was nothing much in my new neighbourhood other than empty spaces and a few sad-looking grocery stores. That's when Mrs Jolly, the friendly proprietor of a small bakery I frequented, directed me towards Edmonton. I had stopped by the building on my way back home from work one day. The signboard in front screamed, 'Enjoy a Canadian Shopping Experience at Edmonton Shopping Mall.'

With a large part of my family settled in Canada, I was thrilled to find something that would remind me of them, drive away the initial pangs of homesickness. I remember running out of the car and into the building hoping to find all my favourite haunts there—Tim Hortons, Reitmans, SuperStore, Chapters. Imagine my dismay when I found the mall empty. There was a small shop in the corner selling Kashmiri handicrafts. On my way out I asked the guard at the entrance why the mall was abandoned. 'Madamji, the shops haven't opened yet. Come back in a few months.'

It's been nineteen years. Edmonton Shopping Mall hardly has any shops other than a few offices of real estate agencies. It's been overshadowed by the newer kids on the block—Ambience, DLF City Centre, MGF Metropolitan. The Canadian NRI population who had bought a huge chunk of real estate when Gurgaon was being developed two decades back have either sold or rented out their properties to the newer immigrants of the Millennium City.

While the older portions of the city have clung to their Indian roots with names such as Rajiv Nagar, Shivaji Nagar, Ashok Vihar, newer parts of globalization-ravaged Gurgaon are still labouring under the illusion (or should I say delusion) that it is a *phoren* city. Just like Singapore.

Now if you will excuse me. I have been invited to tea at a house in Tulip Lane next door. That to me is straight out of Enid Blyton's *Faraway Tree* series. I wonder whether the person in charge of naming roads in our neighbourhood is an Enid Blyton fan, unlikely as it may sound. I wonder whether Moon-Face and Dame Washalot will be there too!

Work

A Thumb for a Thumb!
Just what the Guru ordered.

1.
Mrs Invisible

I'm sorry but I don't have much faith in the figures our Census puts out. I'm talking about the 'Great Invisible Force' of sixteen crore jobless women that was reported in the papers a couple of days ago. A significant proportion of working age group women are confined to their home and hearth doing domestic chores because the society and economic policies have failed them. It makes me want to throw in the towel and weep. Not just because I feel sorry for these women and the opportunities that might have passed them by (I genuinely feel their pain) but also because I might have been counted as one of them!

Yes, that's what I have been reduced to. A statistical report, and an incorrect one at that. I'm quite sure there are many others such as me, similarly infuriated when the headlines hit them on the face. Not that there is anything wrong with looking after the home and hearth. I spend a lot of my time doing that too! But in between cooking, doing the laundry and trying to provide the right environment for my daughter, I follow my dreams and earn money too. It's not a hell of a lot but I do get by.

Only the beady-eyed man who came visiting my house collecting Census data did not seem to think so. Wait till I get my hands on him.

To begin with, the manner in which he rang the doorbell, several times in quick succession, ticked me off much before I actually laid eyes on him. Almost as though I'm supposed to drop whatever it is that I am doing and rush to the door because a 'Very Important Person Designated For Government Work' is calling.

After taking in my dishevelled appearance (complete with a shabby tee and a shabbier pair of Bermuda shorts), he ordered me to get him a glass of water, heading straight into the house without opening his shoes. I stared after him angrily, sputtering in rage. You see, whenever I am really angry I find that words fail me and, and I am not particularly polite to strangers. But you can blame my mother for that. She drilled a deep sense of mistrust with respect to strangers when I was little.

Well, this particular stranger certainly deserved my mistrust.

After plonking himself on my dining table without invitation and roughly pushing my laptop aside to give himself space, he took out a sheaf of papers from a brown case and started copiously taking notes.

Then the questions started. In Hindi.

After asking how many people lived in the house, along with their names, ages and relationships, he proceeded to ask about how we earned our living. 'Do you own this flat or is it rented?' I couldn't help but smile at this question. If each part of the country had a favourite question, this would be North India's top one. Everyone, including my neighbour to the *sabzi wallah* has asked me this!

After enquiring about my husband's job, he looked at me dismissively, having already made up his mind.

Mr Beady-Eyed Census Man: You are a housewife, right?

Me (irritable): No, I work.

Mr Beady-Eyed Census Man: Where do you work? (looking me up and down while he said that.)

Me (snappy): I work from home.

Mr Beady-Eyed Census Man (impatiently, clucking his tongue against his teeth): Yes I know, you do housework at home but where is your office?

Me (Shouting): No, I mean my office is at home. I work from home. I am a journalist, I write articles and reports.

Mr Beady-Eyed Census Man (getting up to leave): Yes, that's very nice. You like to write. But that isn't a job. That's a hobby that you do in your spare time. You paint, you sing, you write. You need to go to an office to work. Doing housework isn't really work and I can't list a hobby as a profession.

The last thing I remember was the metal door clanging shut after him. I might have had a seizure or collapsed, I don't really remember. I do know that I hadn't throttled him. Nothing had been reported in the newspapers the next day.

Beady's alive and kicking. And we have our Census figures to prove it.

I have slipped into oblivion with one stroke of Beady's pen. All my hard work of twelve years wasted. I am a part of the Invisible Work Force. For people such as Beady, creatures like me are mutants. Not to be acknowledged on paper. A home is a home and work is work. Work from home is housework and work from an office is a profession. There is no mixing the two. And you know what the worst part is? I know he's not the only one. There are many, many Beadys out there. God save us!

2.

Waterlogged

A village by any other name would still be...a village! Shakespeare didn't write that. I made that up.

The Government of Haryana has recently renamed Gurgaon to Gurugram to preserve its rich historical heritage and rekindle the Drona connection. Legend has it that Gurgaon was actually 'guru gram', the ancestral village of the warrior mystic Guru Dronacharya who taught military arts to the Pandavas and Kauravas.

Epic news, but no one is happy about it.

Instead, everyone is crying foul about the name change, in real life as well as on social media. I don't understand what the fuss is about. It was a village before. It's still a village, right? From gaon to gram, has anything really changed? Perhaps now we will stop giving ourselves airs and graces, dump the Millennium City tag permanently and focus on the rustic nature of our surroundings?

Everyone around me has been prattling on about Gurgaon being in the running for the Smart City Challenge announced by Prime Minister Narendra Modi recently. What absolute nonsense! News like this really perplexes me. Who in their right minds would consider Gurgaon, erm, Gurugram, to be a smart city? I've been living in this place for well over nineteen years and I can't think of one good reason that would help it qualify.

Fancy buildings, fancy malls, hell even fancy people do not make a Smart City. I wouldn't look like a twenty-year-old if I dyed my hair black now, would I? Poor example aside, I hope the Haryana government is aware of that. Despite the posh facade which, in the words of my neighbour Mrs Chopra, is 'just like Singapore no?' Gurgaon is nothing more than a village. A very fancy village, if you please.

Does Singapore have roads like ours? Ghastly, uneven, potholed—hardly more than dirt tracks in some places. You need to be in the mood for serious adventure sports if you are driving through Gurgaon. Think dirt-track racing! There are no pavements or zebra crossings for pedestrians. Traffic lights don't work. Why, even street lights don't work and traffic guards are missing in action at important junctions. I caught one the other day having a cup of tea while pandemonium had erupted on the streets. It took me a whole lot of self-control not to grab him by the scruff of his neck and fling him in front of rush hour traffic. Every second person, like me, has anger management issues. You can't really blame us.

Every day, there are man-made disasters waiting to happen. You just hope Lady Luck is smiling at you when you leave the house in the morning. Don't even get me started on the natural disasters bit. Gurgaon is a high-risk seismic zone and we live in fear of the occasional rumble. The concrete towers that have mushroomed all across the Village aren't really earthquake-proof you know. My daughter probably puts more thought into her Lego block buildings. There isn't a disaster management system in place either. One heavy earthquake and we will all crumble to dust. And I'm not being dramatic.

It's said that if you dig deep, you can find your soul. In Gurgaon's case, not much digging is required. The rains have

Waterlogged 149

washed away the fancy shmancy exterior and all that remains is the dirt and muddy water. Everywhere you look, miles and miles of it. Last monsoon, a busy road caved in near my house, creating a Niagara Falls type situation. Traffic was held up for hours on end and people gathered at the spot to gawk and click photographs.

The situation hasn't improved.

It's raining as I write this piece. In fact, it's been raining incessantly the whole day. I've waded through dirty water to buy bread and eggs from the grocery shop downstairs, get my daughter from the bus stop outside our condominium and withdraw money from the ATM. It seems as though I've been wading through ick the whole day. And I haven't even stepped out onto the main road!

My building, like many others, is waterlogged. The parking lots are overflowing with mucky water. There's water inside the lift in the next block of flats. We have stores, a doctor's clinic and an ATM inside our complex—all part of the plan to have modern, self-contained buildings. But what good are shops and ATMs if you have to swim to reach them? Thank heavens, my parents taught me how to swim when I was a child. I'm sure they didn't intend for me to be using my skills this way though.

It's worse outside. The roads and highways are flooded, there are traffic snarls across the Village and people are stuck in their cars unable to get to their offices. Tempers are rising. There are rumours doing the rounds about people ordering pizzas from their cars. I wouldn't be surprised if those rumours were actually true. I'm thinking of ordering one myself right now.

What a shame! The behind-the-scenes story of Gurgaon, India's Millennium City, booming industrial hub which is coming apart at the seams without proper drainage, infrastructure or electricity. Every time there is a downpour, life comes to a standstill. Perhaps, as one bloke posted on Twitter, it's time to invest in a boat rather than get another car. I bet it's all part of an ingenious plan to model Gurgaon along the lines of a European city. One that requires the use of gondolas? I mean, if Kolkata could be London, why can't Gurgaon be Venice?

Can gondolas be bought online though? I just remembered. I can't step outside as it's waterlogged.

I mean no disrespect to Indian villages in this piece, some of which are more modern than the one I'm living in now.

3.

Friday Dressing

Today is Friday, it is my day to live a simple life
Put on my make-up, dress up in color
Maybe you might see me down here

(Goldspot)

Last week, I was on my way to a meeting at a leading multinational in Gurgaon. Well ahead of time, I parked my car at the basement parking lot and headed towards the elevators at a leisurely pace taking in the sights, sounds (and smells) of the eatery complex the building was located in. There were crowds of people in brightly-coloured clothes all around me who, I assumed, were heading towards a meal at one of the many restaurants nearby.

It was Friday afternoon and there was a relaxed air about the place as though everyone was getting ready to let their hair down after a long week. I could see the twinkling lights and illuminated signboards of the eateries in the distance and strains of music wafted towards me as I waited in the spacious lobby for the lift to arrive.

I was a bit taken aback when a gaggle of youngsters ran into the elevator with me. They were a young bunch, barely in their twenties and suddenly, the lift was filled with the sound of giggles and the smell of perfume. 'Were there more restaurants upstairs?' I wondered, squeezed into the far recesses of the metal box by the jovial youngsters. It seemed unlikely as the nameplates in the lobby downstairs had indicated offices. And some more. Perhaps I had missed out on a cafeteria or a bar. Where on earth were these kids headed?

Imagine my surprise when the lift came to a halt at the eighth floor and the youngsters stepped out and walked towards the glass doors of the office my meeting was scheduled at. I followed them, keeping a safe distance. It looked as though they were employees. How distinctly odd. They were dressed for an evening out, not for a day at work.

'Ms Gooptu!' a lady in a voluminous, garishly printed maxi was advancing towards me with a smile. Shaking off my temporary befuddlement at the sight of the blue and green printed flowers on her bosom, I smiled at her. 'I'm Shefali,' the maxi lady announced. 'We've spoken a few times over the phone. I've seen your picture on Twitter and so I recognized you.'

I grinned, my eyes widening in recognition and shook the hand she had extended towards me.

She pointed towards the brown leather sofas in the reception area. 'You are slightly early. Perhaps you'd like to wait over there? I will gather the team and call you in soon.'

'*Humma, Humma,*' the golden coloured phone in her hand had burst into melody. It was the tune of a popular Hindi film song. She spoke impatiently into the mouthpiece before flouncing off down the corridor, the printed folds of her maxi flying around her, stiletto heels going *clickety clack*.

I stared after her in astonishment. I'd never seen anyone wearing a printed maxi in an office before. She looked as though she was headed to a summer lunch party with her pals. Friday casuals were one thing and today was a Friday, I'll give her that. But this took casual to a whole new dimension altogether.

When I was ushered into my meeting several minutes later, I realized, much to my horror, that she wasn't the only one.

Everyone in the tiny conference room we were packed in was wearing brightly-coloured beach shirts, voluminous shimmery gowns, fluorescent tops in yellow and green, geometric prints, flowing skirts, metallic jackets and precarious high heels. It was almost as though a fashion show had gone horribly wrong. I was in the middle of Project Runway Horror Show! The mothers I ran into at my daughter's school were better dressed. Good grief, I couldn't believe that I was in the offices of a prominent international conglomerate.

I found myself unable to concentrate on the meeting or the slides of the PowerPoint presentation that were being flashed on the LCD screen, one after another. A man in a bright green Hawaiian shirt was managing the slide show with a commentary on each of them. His shabby denims were paired with sandals that made a soft swish sound each time he paced the room while making the presentation.

I kept staring at the people around me and pinching myself at intervals, surreptitiously, over the formal blue blazer I was wearing. But this wasn't a bad dream and the pinches really hurt. These people were as real as the droplets of condensation on the tiny Bisleri water bottles that had been placed in front of us.

I have since then learnt my lesson. The lesson being that workwear is an outdated concept in Gurgaon. People in Gurgaon follow their own (rather peculiar) dress code at workplaces. The employees of the office I had been to were not deviants. Rather, they were the norm. I have visited many offices over the course of the last two years and each of these experiences have been a tad more bizarre than the previous.

Having spent almost a decade working from home, I guess I was completely out of touch with the modern workwear code in Gurgaon, which can be described as 'Go as You Like.' From personal experiences and anecdotes shared by people I know, it would seem as though Friday dressing or should I say, everyday dressing, has been taken over by 'are you out of your mind' dressing.

Perhaps it's just as well. No one can accuse employers of forcing employees to adhere to unreasonable dress codes. If one wears stilettos of one's own free will, there shouldn't be any problem. Of course, if I were an employer, I might have complained about my employees' outlandish dress sense. But that's not happening anytime soon, is it? So I'd better get used to it. Or perhaps go for some outlandish dressing myself?

Time to invest in a frilly maxi perhaps or a fluorescent tank top?

4.

Drive to Hell

My ride to office this morning could have been Michael Schumacher in another life. A thin, frail-looking chap with a blue cap on his head that said 'Champ' raced his black and yellow auto down the pothole-ridden roads of Gurgaon, manoeuvering the craters and tumultuous traffic effortlessly as though we were on one of the Formula One circuits. All this while, I clung on to the metal rails by my side, the frayed plastic from the padding overhead flapping against my face, clenched my teeth and prayed to God to help me reach my destination in one piece. Loud music blared from the tiny speakers positioned somewhere within the vehicle. I could make out it was a Bengali song, though I had never heard anything like it before in my life. Roughly translated, the lyrics went thus:

Oh wearer of jeans pant,
Tell me what your name is,
Your shampooed locks are a lure for me,
If you're travelling to Kolkata,
Please take me with you!

I'm sure anyone who has (safely) completed a journey in this vehicle will not have been in any state to go to Kolkata, leave alone anywhere else. If this was what minutes before death felt like, it was certainly not pleasant. I could feel the insides of my stomach turn. I wished I had not eaten the scrambled eggs for breakfast. I clutched the rail tighter, squeezed my eyes shut and prayed some more. I could hear the noise from the traffic around me getting louder. Deafening.

I survived. But that's not the crux of this story.

Commuting in and around Gurgaon is a nightmare. There is no organized system of public transport. Most people drive their own cars and if you don't, you are in for some really nasty surprises in the form of rented cabs, autos and cycle rickshaws. Autos are to be avoided if you have a weak heart and low tolerance for horrendous music! But I'm stuck with the latter as I don't have much faith in Meru, Uber or Ola either. The Meru driver fell asleep while driving the last cab I hired. Thankfully, the car came to a halt in the middle of the road and we narrowly missed a nasty accident though I'm still recovering from the trauma. Talk about being between a rock and a hard place.

Most of the chaps (outsourced from Bengal and Bihar) who drive these beastly autos don't go by the meter and you have to cough up whatever their whim dictates at that very moment. Or refuse, stick your nose up in the air and walk to your destination in a huff, which means walking five miles to get to your office. So, you just swallow your pride, accept your lousy luck and sign up for the scariest journey of your life, praying that you come out of it, unscathed and alive!

I'm really not sure how I managed the feat, mostly by the skin of my teeth perhaps, but I made a mental note never to get on an auto again. Perhaps it would have made better sense to have headed straight to a car showroom and spent all my savings on a new car, then and there.

When I finally stumbled into office, an hour or so later, all dishevelled, my colleague, a pretty twenty-something walked up

Drive to Hell

to me with a tall glass of water. 'Arre, what's the matter? Why do you look so...' she paused, searching for the right word. English was not one of her strengths. 'Agitated!' she said triumphantly after a second. 'Are you all right?'

'No, I'm not all right,' I said, huffing and puffing, drawing deep breaths as I gulped down the water. 'I don't have any transport and coming to office is becoming a nightmare each day.'

She looked concerned. 'Oh dear, that doesn't sound good,' she said, her brows knitted in concentration. 'But I may have just the solution for you,' she added. 'You need a Jugnu. Why don't you book a Jugnu to take you home since you don't have transport?'

I gaped at her, horrified. What on earth was she talking about? What an outrageous suggestion.

She quickly clarified, 'Arre it's a new app for booking auto rides. You can book an auto on your smartphone. The vehicles are better-maintained and the drivers are more professional. Besides, they go by the meter. So you end up paying much less for a smoother ride.'

I heaved a sigh of relief. Well, thank heavens for that. It wasn't quite as scandalous as it sounded. Book a Jugnu indeed.

I feel like Rip Van Winkle these days. Perhaps I should go back to sleep again.

5.
All the Village Is an App

In Gurgaon, every second person you run into is a start-up founder who has designed an app.

While that spells good news for innovation and the state of burgeoning business in the Millennium City, it makes life extremely tiresome for ordinary people like me.

The other day, I was settling down in front of my laptop at the co-working space which I share with several other folks like me without a permanent office to call their own. The space, in question, is a charming, three-storeyed building close to my house at the end of a secluded, tree-lined avenue. Each floor has several workstations, a small pantry and a washroom. There are motivational quotations framed on the bright yellow and green walls and a diminutive office boy is on call throughout the day to get you unlimited refills of tea and coffee from a vending machine down the hall. It has all the makings of an idyllic workplace.

Except that it isn't one.

My co-workers are a motley bunch of people. There are freelance writers, chartered accountants, small business owners, researchers, public relations consultants and last but certainly not the least, start-up founders—the root cause of all my troubles.

'Excuse me,' I heard a voice addressing me. I looked up from my laptop and noticed that a really tall man had appeared in front of me. I had never seen him before at the office. He was clean-shaven with a smooth, swarthy complexion, shiny black hair plastered to his skull. I noticed that he was quite good-looking in a South Indian movie star sort of way. He was wearing a Hawaiian print shirt and cargo shorts. His feet were in black sandals.

'Is this seat taken?' he pointed to the empty chair next to me, where I had dumped my laptop bag. His tone was amiable but his voice was really loud. I saw several of my co-workers stare in our direction. There were several empty chairs scattered around the room and I had no idea why he had zeroed in on this particular one.

'No,' I said, watching him warily as he pulled out the chair, placed the bag on the table and purposefully sat down facing me.

'Can I take a bit of your time? I wanted to ask you some questions.'

Now, I didn't want to seem rude and the man wasn't really giving me much of a choice. So I nodded. Secretly I was hoping he would notice the mutinous expression that had clouded my face, get up and leave. He didn't. He just droned on.

'Allow me to introduce myself, Ma'am. My name is Sukumar Swamy. I am a start-up founder,' the man said, sending an errant strand of hair back to his scalp with flourish.

Over the next hour, Sukumar Swamy informed me that he had recently relocated from Mumbai, sold his old e-commerce business and developed a fitness app named F-I-T-R and was close to securing millions in funding from a renowned venture capitalist firm in Singapore. He was now conducting market research on the state of fitness in Gurgaon where he had decided to launch the app and would be delighted if I could help answer some questions that he had relating to women and fitness.

I groaned and all but slumped into my chair. What was it

about me that attracted all these fitness types? First the runners and now the app designers.

Swamy stared at me as though he expected me to break out into a jig with excitement at the thought of being the chosen one. It was hilarious, I thought. He couldn't have chosen a better subject for his market research. I was, without doubt, the most unfit person in the office, leave alone the Village. If he based his research on an interview with me, his app was doomed.

That may have been a pleasant thought to mull over but the next hour certainly wasn't. Swamy asked me question after question. I fielded all of them somewhat patiently while he took notes copiously, nodding his head at intervals.

After the interview was over, he leaned back on the chair, palms at the back of his head and contemplated the ceiling for several minutes. Then he sprang from the chair, shook my hand and said, 'It's been very informative talking to you, Ma'am. Do tell your friends about my app. I will keep you posted about the launch date.' With that, he strode out of the office briskly, the sound of his slippers going flap all the way down the stairs. Good riddance, I thought to myself.

Long after he had completed his impromptu interview and left, I could see the other start-up guys in the office eyeing me interestedly, much like one would look at a lab rat before getting them ready for an experiment. I hurriedly dumped my laptop inside the bag and exited the building before someone else grabbed me. I decided to spend the rest of the day working at the nearest coffee shop.

But where do I go, where do I hide? Even the coffee shops that I frequent are full of them.

After the Sukumar Swamy experience, I've become a seeker. I can spot them from a distance. You will usually find them sitting together in a group, talking very loudly. The subject of their conversation is usually venture capitalists, investors and term sheets. Though by the end of it, you almost wish it was a charge sheet for their obnoxious behaviour and someone would arrest them and put them behind bars.

Most of them have designed a really cool app that will change the face of the earth. Or so they claim. You wish they would have designed an app that would help them dress better, or be more polite. People in India make a huge deal about women being improperly attired at work or at public places. Why don't the same rules apply for men? Why can't these start-up types dress decently when they are going to work? I don't turn up for work in a bathing suit, do I? I find it offensive when men land up to work in shorts and chappals. I don't care a hoot if you have invented an app. We are not on a beach so cover up, for God's sake.

I had just ordered some coffee and found myself a comfortable seat near the window when someone tapped me on my shoulder. There was a man standing next to me. He was short with a tonsured head. His beady eyes bore into mine with a strange intensity. 'Excuse me, can I speak with you for a minute? I've designed a homework app. Do you have any children?'

6.
I Hunger for You

Ever since I stopped working from home and set up my office in a co-working space, I've got into a relationship and it's complicated.

Life at home was simple—three meals a day, cooked by a merry-faced woman from West Bengal. Steamed rice, fish curry, dal and vegetables and perhaps the odd chicken or lamb in the evenings or over the weekends. Edible but unexciting. Safe but boring as hell.

Working out of an office has changed all of that. My fling is taking a toll on my emotional and physical well-being. I am cranky most of the time, looking at my phone furtively whenever I get a chance, and falling into the guilt trap every now and then. All of the usual symptoms that one would associate with an affair.

Breaking up is never easy to do but I've decided to take a call. I need to end the affair once and for all. My sanity is at stake.

Do you remember that scene in *Sex and the City* where Carrie threw her phone into the ocean so that she wouldn't have to speak to her estranged fiancé Mr Big anymore? I am that close to throwing my phone away so that I am not tempted anymore. The thing that stops me is the fact that Gurgaon is miles away from the ocean. There isn't even a decent puddle nearby and I'm not up for a two-hour drive to the Jamuna. Besides, I'm not a character in a book. I'm a writer and I don't think I can afford to throw a phone into the sea.

So I have to do the next best thing. Delete all the food apps from my phone.

Oh! Did you think I was having an affair with an actual person? Wipe that look off your face right now.

Food apps have made my life a living hell. I am having a relationship, many actually, with the multitude of food apps that are crowding my phone. Two-timing one with the other. Ordering breakfast from one and then lunch from another. Sinful right? Not to mention double-crossing, sly and manipulative.

What can I do? What would you do if you woke up to a message promising gastronomic delights. Sausages, salami, ham, scrambled eggs, bacon, beans, brioche, croissants, all with a swipe of your finger. And just when you were being faithful to one app, another would pop up tempting you to stray into forbidden territory. Hunan chicken, Burritos, Roulades, Peri Peri grilled Basa with vegetables and crispy fried potatoes, Piri Piri Pomfret, Chicken noodles with gravy. Before you could click your way out, they would be offering you dessert. Blueberry cheesecake, red velvet brownie, gulab jamuns, eclairs. Oh wait, there was even a salted caramel chocolate tart as a freebie.

Now, I don't have that kind of self-control. So I have caved in. Months and months of cheating with guilt and self-loathing have brought me to a point where there seems to be no turning back.

You see, work from home doesn't give one the option of eating homely meals at work ordered from food apps. I'm in a whole new zone altogether. The merry-faced cook from West Bengal seems an apparition. Instead, there are uniformed delivery boys who bring neatly packed containers stuffed with deliciousness.

Only now, the aches and pains are not mental anymore. My joints ache, my fingers hurt and I have started swelling up like the little girl in *Charlie and the Chocolate Factory*. The one who turned into a blueberry. It is not a pleasant sight. One trip to the doctor and I have been given the ultimatum. It is uric acid that has done the snitching. Damn!

Get back on the straight and narrow. Or else. A glare from the doctor and my defenses have crumbled. My cheeks are flushed and I have the look of a deer caught in the headlights. It's not nice being found out.

What do I do? It is painful. Separation always is. But it has to be done. Swiftly and mercilessly.

It feels strange to look at my phone nowadays. I miss them, those bright little widgets promising such deliciousness, forbidden pleasures. I fantasize about them sometimes. But I won't go down that self-destructive path again. I feel strangely empty too and there's a gnawing sensation at the pit of my stomach.

Oh wait, that's probably hunger. Let me go and have a cracker.

And though breaking up is hard to do
I wouldn't give our love one more try!

7.
Parking Games

My neighbour Mr Chopra was inconsolable. His brand new silver-grey Audi had been stolen from the road outside his office. He had left it there in the morning on the way to work. On his way back home for lunch he noticed that the car had disappeared. Not a soul knew where it had vanished. Even the paanwala who sat across the road from the office building was blank. He hadn't seen anything suspicious. The police hadn't been of much help either. 'We will look into it,' they had told him curtly. Adding, 'You should have been more careful sirji. Incidents of car thefts across Gurgaon are on the rise. Surely you read about them in the papers. Why did you leave your car outside on the road?'

Mr Chopra didn't have an answer.

When I heard the sad story from an ashen-faced Mrs Chopra the next morning, I couldn't help but feel that the chap deserved having his car stolen. In fact, he had been asking for it.

Several weeks ago, the Chopras invited me out to go watch a movie with them. Since my husband was travelling and I had been cooped up at home for a week, Mrs Chopra thought it was a good idea for me to accompany the couple to watch the latest Hrithik Roshan potboiler being shown at the movie theatres. Now, I am not a particular fan of Hrithik but the movie was rumoured to be an epic tale about Mohenjo Daro and the Harappan Civilization. That period of history has always fascinated me and I was willing to put aside my dislike of Hrithik for a couple of hours to accommodate my love for all things historical.

We headed towards the multiplex movie theatre at the nearest mall in order to have an early dinner at the food court and watch the movie afterwards. Mr Chopra had bought the tickets online so there was nothing much to do other than reach the venue on time. We piled into Mr Chopra's new car, bought to announce his change of jobs, and set off.

Just as we were nearing the mall, I noticed Mr Chopra slowing down and getting ready to park the car alongside a long line of vehicles parked on the main road outside the mall.

'Why are you parking the car here?' I asked. 'Why don't you park inside the mall. It's much safer there.'

Mr Chopra coughed and turned off the ignition. 'Are you crazy?' he stared at me as though I had escaped from the lunatic asylum. 'Why would I park inside the mall?'

'Everyone parks their car inside. They have two floors of parking and it's so convenient. Why would you park here?' I insisted. 'Besides, this is on the main road. There will be a logjam in seconds and we are blocking the traffic on the main road.' I couldn't believe anyone could be so irresponsible.

Mr Chopra looked thunderous. Mrs Chopra tapped me gently on the shoulder. 'We always park here. It's the weekend and parking fees are so expensive. Why waste all that money parking inside when you can park here for free. Much better, no?'

'But your car might get towed away if it's illegally parked,' I cried.

'Nahi,' Mr Chopra said. 'The Gurgaon Police don't have cranes to tow away cars. No one will touch my car. Let's go!'

I sighed. I could see that he wouldn't budge. I saw well-dressed couples with families alighting from the fancy cars that were parked alongside the Chopras' Audi. Clearly, they were also scrimping on the weekend parking fees. How much again would that have cost them? Fifty bucks at the most? And how much did these fancy cars cost? In lakhs?

I walked to the mall trailing behind the couple, with a mutinous expression on my face. It was dark and I'm sure they hadn't noticed. I made a mental note never to accompany them for a movie ever again. The movie was a disaster, an epic failure partly due to the fact that I was really put-off by the entire parking episode and couldn't pay attention to what was happening on-screen.

If you have enough money to buy a Mercedes or an Audi, shouldn't you be able to spare the small change for mall parking fees? Why on earth would you create a traffic snarl on the road outside so that you wouldn't have to pay for parking?

If all of Gurgaon's errant car owners get their cars nicked, there wouldn't be reason to have one day of the week without cars. Every day would be car-free. There wouldn't be any cars left.

Perfect punishment for the penny wise, pound foolish.

Play

Keep Calm and Let the Games Begin.

1.

Doing Coffee

Friend: Why don't we do coffee this weekend?

Me: Sorry, I don't do coffee. In fact, I don't 'do' anything really.

Friend: Really?

Me: No no, I don't mean I don't do anything. I work, I'm a writer. I don't do beverages. I drink them. I drink tea actually. Could do with a cup right now.

The truth is I never really drank coffee till I moved to Gurgaon, nineteen years ago. Growing up in Kolkata, all I knew about coffee was the Nescafé sachets that were occasionally spotted in the bag of groceries when a coffee-drinking relative or friend was visiting. Like most Bengali families, ours was fastidious about tea. Darjeeling tea had to be and brewed for exactly five minutes in a ceramic Bengal Pottery teapot. Coffee was a vile, strong-smelling, muddy liquid that guests drank when they visited. Or even my older siblings when they were pulling an all-nighter before their examinations.

Gurgaon changed all that. People didn't drink tea here. At least not the kind of tea I was used to. In this part of the country, tea leaves were boiled with milk and sugar in a saucepan well past boiling point. Often, cardamom and other assorted aromatics were chucked into the milky broth to make a fragrant stew. I only drank the liquid once at a friend's place, fooled into believing it was tea.

I still wince when I'm reminded of that agonizing instance when the foul drink had entered my mouth. I couldn't spit it out. So I sat there, with a fixed smile on my face, hurriedly gulping down the scalding brew. Or should I say stew. I had vowed then and there never to drink tea outside my own home again.

But what could I do? Gurgaon stores didn't sell Darjeeling tea. At least they didn't nineteen years ago. It's different now, with all the fancy supermarkets, tea boutiques and websites peddling different, exotic varieties of tea. Those days, the shopkeeper in the neighbourhood kirana store would look at you strangely if you asked for Darjeeling tea.

Shopkeeper: Darjeeling? Isn't that a hill station somewhere in the east?

Me: Yes yes, but you also get very good tea there. World-famous tea actually.

Shopkeeper: Really? Never heard of it.

After a couple of unsuccessful, frustrating excursions to the local markets, I did the next best thing. I made sure my cupboards were stocked with packets of my favourite brand of Darjeeling tea (procured throughout the year while visiting Kolkata or as gifts from friends and relatives). There was peace in my life again.

Till coffee happened.

It was the end of the '90s. Coffee shops had mushroomed all over the Village as international brands tried to find a foothold in the promising new market. It started with Barista, followed by Café Coffee Day, Costa Coffee, The Coffee Bean and Tea Leaf and then, the flashy new entrant, Starbucks Coffee. Coffee shops became de rigueur. It was hip and fashionable to 'do' coffee. Or chai latte (what an abomination of a drink!) in a coffee shop. All of a sudden, my girlfriends and mommy friends were calling me up to set up coffee dates.

Suddenly, it wasn't quite as simple as a Nescafé sachet anymore!

'Let's do coffee this week,' my friends would say. 'We will sit and chit-chat over a cup.'

'But I don't drink coffee,' I would argue.

'Don't be ridiculous! I'm sure there is something there that you can drink,' they would insist.

They were right, of course. There was much more than just coffee.

There was espresso, cappuccino, latte, macchiato and what-have-yous. Iced, warm, topped with whipped cream, ice cream, chocolate sauce, chocolate shavings and any other edible thing that caught one's fancy. Refined sugar, demerara sugar, sugar-free. Tall glasses, short glasses, styrofoam cups, tumblers. It was all quite fascinating. Only I couldn't get myself to like coffee. And the tea they served (as an after thought) wasn't Darjeeling. There was green tea, breakfast tea, Earl Grey, Assam, Hibiscus, Jasmine, Chamomile, Oolong. Exotic, fragrant and alien! Still, the mind-boggling array of food on display more than made up for it.

I would tag along happily, on most days, to eat a sandwich, a chicken lattice or a gigantic slice of New York cheesecake while the others 'did' coffee and gossiped to their heart's content. Alongside devouring all the juicy bits about people's personal lives, I was also piling on calories in the process.

The coffee shops also doubled up as workplaces. So, in addition to 'doing' coffee, you could also do work, have a meeting with your office colleagues, get funding for your new business, read a book, write one or spend hours browsing the Internet for free if you had nothing better to do.

Over the course of my visits to Gurgaon's coffee shops, I would find executive types hunched over their laptops, kitty party groups, singletons near the window poring into a book with a cup of coffee and a solitary muffin on a plate, or expat mothers socializing over steaming cups of coffee with babies in sling bags.

Some days, I would find a gaggle of school kids (playing hookey no doubt) giggling furtively as they huddled together drinking iced coffee out of tall glasses.

I found it very interesting to watch this assortment of people as they assembled under one roof to drink coffee, wondering how their real lives were, what they were talking about or working on, where they were headed next. Was that young couple squabbling over something? Was the lady by the window writing a book? Did that young man just get a job? Each day was a new episode of a television serial that unfolded right in front of my eyes. I was getting addicted. Not to the beverage, but the ambience.

The other day, I spotted my neighbour Mrs Malhotra 'doing' coffee with her daughter's swimming instructor. I wouldn't have known who she was had our daughters not been swimming in the same pool. She lives in the same condominium complex as me, is most likely in her early thirties and stunning to look at. I've noticed the instructor at the poolside training the young children. He's a good-looking Jat boy and a hot favourite with the mummies. From the look of it, this mummy too! It was winter so I don't think they were discussing swimming lessons. The glances that were being exchanged between the two were steamier than the smoke from the mugs in front of them. I think they were doing a lot more than coffee, in real life. My television serial had just gotten more interesting. But more about that another day.

Whoever said that a lot can happen over coffee was obviously right. Gurgaon's coffee shops had certainly proved that. They haven't converted me to a coffee aficionado yet but I have found the middle ground in hot chocolate with whipped cream. Clearly, there's still hope for me.

Coffee anyone?

2.

Run for Your Life

Someone asked me at a party the other day whether I ran. The lady in question was a svelte, thirty-something, all shiny and toned, dressed in the most exquisite of clothes. She would have given Deepika Padukone a complex.

'Excuse me?' I asked. Maybe I hadn't heard right.

'I was asking whether you ran? I mean, are you part of any running group here in Gurgaon?' she asked.

I stared at her incredulously. Were her eyes alright, I wondered. She didn't have glasses on, but perhaps she had contact lenses hidden in those sparkly pupils? I scanned her face to see if she was blinking one too many times. Didn't seem like it. No blinks at all. She was definitely not all right up there in the head then, I thought nastily to myself. What a peculiar question to ask someone you've just met. Did I look like a person who ran? Most mornings, I got out of breath just walking up to the front door from my bed to get the newspapers.

I leaned closer to her with a strange gleam in my eyes. 'The only time I run is when someone is chasing me. Like a zombie for instance,' I whispered. Her sparkly eyes nearly popped out of their sockets. 'Whaaaat?' she gasped.

'Don't tell anyone,' I added, leaning even closer. 'But I believe the zombie apocalypse is around the corner. They are going to take over our planet you know. I've even spotted a few lurking about my condominium complex in the evenings!'

The woman turned pale. She slowly set her drink down on the table in front of us, managed a sheepish smile and excused herself. After that, she made sure she maintained a safe distance from me for the rest of the party. I spotted her whispering to her husband, pointing over in my direction, when dinner was being served. He looked as though he had spent a serious amount of time building his body, toned pecs bursting beneath the sheer black shirt. Our eyes met over the dinner table and he looked away. I wonder what she had told him.

While I feel slightly ashamed of my behaviour towards her, zombies are a perfectly good excuse to stay away from Gurgaon's rapidly growing fitness brigade. Fitness is the latest fad to have seized the Millennium City carpe diem style and the growing ranks of fitness freaks are an alarming development for people like me. Let's just say that I'm probably more prepared for a zombie apocalypse than a fitness one!

The fitness brigade walk, run, cycle and exercise religiously every day. They eat healthy and frown at almost anything that isn't organic or pesticide-free. And if that isn't enough, they work hard to convert everyone (who isn't so inclined) to their way of life. If there was a choice between zombies and fitness fanatics taking over the earth, I would totally root for the zombie takeover. Of course, I'm hoping they would all look like Nicholas Hoult in *Warm Bodies*.

'All that sugar can't be good for you,' one of them remarked casually the other day, just as I was about to bite into a decadent chocolate tart. Not a zombie but a fitness freak.

A group of us were meeting at a neighbourhood café and refreshments had just arrived. My order was the solitary chocolate

176 *Gurgaon Diaries*

truffle tart in the tray full of healthy slushes, chia seed and melon smoothies. I had to applaud her timing. I paused mid-bite guiltily and stared at the woman, a recent convert, who had infiltrated my group of friends. She met my stare, unflinching, and continued relentlessly, wagging perfectly manicured fingers at me, 'I mean, you are over forty aren't you? Shouldn't you be worried about the adverse effects of all that caffeine and refined sugar in your bloodstream?' The other ladies in the group nodded solemnly in agreement.

Well, I hadn't thought about all that sugar in my bloodstream earlier but I, sure as hell, was worried now.

Traitors! I stared at the group of old friends turned foes accusingly and set the tart down slowly. 'I think I'm okay,' I said nonchalantly, trying desperately to think of a witty comeback. The comeback eluded me. 'No, I don't think you are,' the woman continued. 'You should definitely go in for a check-up. Let me know what you find out. I can recommend a good dietician and afterwards, you could join my running group. We meet every morning at 6 a.m. and go for a long run. You can't imagine how good it feels. Try it, I guarantee you will see the results in a week if you join. In fact, all of us are meeting tomorrow morning for a jog. Come no?'

The blood drained from my face as I realized that she had drafted everyone in my group for the jog tomorrow. There were happy smiles being passed around, at the thought of a healthy, fat-free, pesticide-free future. I couldn't share their enthusiasm. I excused myself politely and left, with a heavy heart. Heavy with the grief of losing so many friends in one go. Or perhaps, just heavy with the weight of the refined sugar pressing down on my arteries. I felt a few warning twinges as if the damn organ, my heart, was in agreement with the fitness lady.

That evening, I unfollowed a few more people on social media.

I didn't need to see any more pictures of happy, sweaty people in gym togs on Facebook—perfectly-shaped bodies, gathering in nooks and corners, pursuing their quest for a healthy, fulfilling life. The world of samosas and chocolate tarts was infinitely more exciting for me. Chia and melon seeds could wait along with the tweets on #FitnessforLife. And the only place the vile goos masquerading as health drinks belonged was in animal feed. I sighed, switched off my laptop and got ready to watch *Warm Bodies* on the VCD for the umpteenth time.

As for getting up at five in the morning for a run, there were just four words to express how I felt:

Over my dead body.

3.

Twang, Bang, Thank You Ma'am

'Sharrtullegrundi?'

The young girl behind the counter at the café was smiling at me, fingers paused over the cash register, as she waited for my reply to her question. I had ordered their signature hot chocolate with an extra helping of whipped cream on top and was expecting her to tell me how much the damages were.

I blinked at her. 'Pardon?'

'Sh a r r t u l l e g r u n d i, Madam,' she repeated, slower this time and I could detect the hint of exasperation that had crept into her voice. She was slightly taller than the cash register, sallow complexioned, and I could see her eyes darting over behind me to examine how long the queue had grown. Her white cap bobbed up and down with each movement of her head.

I could feel my cheeks and the tip of my ears turning warmer. 'I'm sorry, I just don't get what you're saying,' I said sheepishly. Did I just imagine it or did the pretty young thing behind me in the queue snigger?

The girl sighed and disappeared behind the counter. She materialized a couple of seconds later holding three, white styrofoam cups with the green café logo emblazoned on them. She held up the cups and pointed to each of them as she said

'Which cup size do you want your hot chocolate in madam? Sharrt, tulle or grundi?'

Suddenly I was back in nursery school again and the teacher was reading out the story of Goldilocks to the class full of noisy children. She was holding up the picture book and pointing to the animals on it: This is Papa Bear, Mama Bear and Baby Bear. Papa Bear is big, Mama Bear medium and Baby Bear is small.

The coffee girl had the same look as my nursery teacher, same tone of voice.

I heaved a sigh of relief. 'Oh, you mean short, tall or grande?' I smiled to hide the embarassment I was feeling.

'Yes,' the coffee girl was looking distinctly annoyed now. 'That's what I said. Sharrt, tulle or grundi! What size do you want?'

I chose my size, paid for the beverage and moved on to the other end of the counter to wait for the hot chocolate to be prepared and served. The pretty young thing and her tall boyfriend sniggered again as I left the queue. The contempt on their faces was unmistakeable. My class, Deciphering Indian Accents 101, was over and I had failed.

While I was familiar with the fact that the café in question was an American chain, I hadn't bargained for the faux American accent I would be getting free of cost along with the American-style beverage I had ordered. Both, as it happens, were actually made in Haryana.

Globalization and the BPO boom have had some annoying side effects in Gurgaon. Haryana now produces a mind-boggling range of accents that would put a language trainer anywhere in the world to shame. From American to Brit to Aussie. That's right mate! Then, there is the unpronounceable, the confused mishmash of twangs from different regions. What I had witnessed at the café. The Haryana meets Hawaii accent. Could have easily been Gurgaon goes to Georgia.

Not just that. Our language these days is liberally peppered with Americanisms.

When we are asked how we are, we say 'We're good.'

When we make mistakes, at times catastrophic ones, we say breezily, 'Oops, my bad.'

We do a 'heads-up' and 'take a call' very often.

We call our female friends 'babes' and do you really need more?

There was a time when students desirous of studying in a foreign country would start speaking in an accent from the time they started picking up prospectuses and application forms. 'Yass ma'am, I wanna stedy in the Kay neigh da,' was a common refrain I remember from my days as an education advisor with the Canadian Education Centre.

Then came the call centres and their employees, the Tom, Dick and Harrys with the rolling r's.

How could I forget Bollywood with its bizarre collection of confused twangs! Priyanka Chopra found her calling in Hollywood, landing a hugely successful television series, thanks to her American twang. That twang certainly came in handy. God knows she had been ribbed for years at home over that accent. Hers was a twangs to riches story.

Nowadays, it's not just the call centres and the Bollywood celebrities. Everyone around me in Gurgaon seems to be spouting the twang. Move over Salman Khan, your time is up. Could it be the Quantico Effect?

Just the other day, a lady created quite a commotion at our neighbourhood grocery store with her twang. She was happily piling up her shopping cart with stuff from the shelves until she hit a snag. *'Mujhe btrrrrrr chahiye,'* she requested a shop boy.

'Kya?' he looked confused.

'Btrrrrr,' repeated the lady. She was dressed in an expensive olive green linen pantsuit, diamonds dripping from her ears, neck and hands. I couldn't believe she was dressed so fancily for a grocery shopping expedition.

'*Woh kya cheez hai?*' the shop boy wasn't being insolent, he just didn't know what she was babbling about. The lady was close to having a hissy fit. She yelled loudly at him and stormed off in a huff, dragging her trolley and leaving a cloud of expensive perfume in the aisles. I could hear her asking to speak to the manager loudly somewhere in the distance. My curiosity was piqued so I walked over casually to the spot where she was standing, pretending all the while to browse for groceries.

The grey-haired manager was baffled.

'Mutter?' he offered helpfully. 'Do you want the peas Madamji? We have several varieties. Fresh, frozen…' he said hesitantly.

'*Mutter nahi btrrrr!*' she was very angry now, eyes flashing, ready to wallop the man with her bag. 'I don't want peas. I want Amul btrrrr! Do you people not understand English here?'

'Ah, b-u-t-t-e-r,' the manager looked relieved, '*toh thik se boliye na*,' pointing towards the cold storage section, behind where I stood. 'You will find it over there.'

The lady stomped off to get her 'bttrr'. I hurriedly moved out of her way, hiding my face so that she wouldn't see I was giggling. I couldn't stop smiling to myself as I went back to my shopping. Wonder where she was from.

Could be from Kay neigh Da. Or perhaps she was an extra from the Quantico set.

4.

Chicken Is the New Black

Last night, on my way to dinner with close friends, I saw a few children attacking what looked like a chicken. As I got closer, I realized that it wasn't actually a chicken but a person inside a chicken suit. Yes, my eyesight is that bad apparently.

The restaurant I was headed to is located in an upscale eatery complex in Gurgaon. It was my friend's birthday and she wanted to treat us at a new restaurant that had just opened its doors to the public. It was an international chain, specializing in exotic, grilled chicken and there were mile-long queues of people waiting to get in, apparently. Now, there are many eateries, coffee shops, fast food joints, pubs and grills located in the zone. The giant bird was loitering outside the restaurant where I was supposed to have dinner.

A few of the kids were poking the chicken while two others kept pulling at his tail feathers. A third infant (in the arms of a maid) was pointing towards the oversized bird and howling incessantly. The bird was cornered!

If you are wondering whether the disciplinarian mother inside me whacked some sense into the naughty kids at once and called their parents out (from somewhere inside the restaurant busy stuffing their mouths) to complain, let me tell you that I didn't.

I simply stood there and stared. I'll tell you why.

Have you ever seen a black chicken before? Well, to be quite honest, I hadn't. It was a cross between a gigantic rooster, chicken and crow all rolled into one. It had a red heart, red comb on its head and an abnormal red plume-like tail. The bizarre oversized bird walked around on its skinny legs doing a little bop once in a while. The spectacle would have given anyone a nightmare really. I'm not surprised that kids were harassing it; the poor baby was frightened out of its wits. They had never seen anything like it either.

While I think it's a great idea for restaurants to have their food parading around in suits, as a lure for customers like they do in the West, a black chicken is a very bad idea, in India at least. Truck drivers would attest to that. You would have seen the trucks on the highway with *Buri Nazar Wale Tera Muh Kala* plastered on the back of the vehicle.

In India, a blackened face is usually associated with ignominy and disgrace. People are shamed when their faces are painted with black ink or when black colour is thrown on them. Take the case of our politicians for instance. They live in fear of the black ink attack. When they are not escaping the shoe hurling that is. It's even a popular curse to ward off the evil eye. 'If you have the evil eye, may your face turn black!' In this country, anything black would hardly be considered the subject of an appetizing meal. The only black bird that we know of is the crow and we don't eat crow. I probably have but more about that later on.

I honestly believe that international food chains should rethink their branding when they set up shop in this country. If you want to make a mark in a new market, you should customize your logo along with customizing your food for the local palate. If McDonald's can do it with McAloo, why can't you?

Though many bird breeders indicate that some varieties of

chicken that are black in colour are known for the superior, gamey quality of meat and eggs. Be that as it may, a black chicken on my plate does not get my taste buds excited. What do you think?

And, if you do have a black chicken parading around your restaurant in a bid to sell flame grilled food, you may actually scare customers away. People aren't familiar with flame grilled food in India. People identify with tandoori chicken and the appetizing reddish brown roasted colour that tandoori food brings to mind. Imagine all the questions in the customer's mind when they look at a black bird:

'What in the hell's name is that?'

'Is it a crow? Is it a rooster? Is it a chicken?'

'Why is it black? Do they sell burnt food here?'

'The menu says it's flame grilled. Did the flame that grilled the bird get so hot that the bird is now char-grilled? Or let's say burnt to a crisp?'

Reminds me of the black bird we used to get served for dinner when we were up all night getting the Budget edition—of a popular business daily in Kolkata—ready. The whole team would get free dinner from the Chinese eatery next door. The menu was always the same—chilli chicken and fried rice. But the bird that came masquerading as chicken each year, doused heavily in soya sauce and vinegar was no chicken. It looked black and inedible. We called it chilli crow instead!

With a heavy heart, I joined my dinner companions inside the restaurant, not looking forward to the meal I was about to be served. I couldn't help feeling sorry for the person inside the bird suit. Poor, unfortunate soul. The things one has to do to earn a living. It might well be his/her last evening at work.

I must clarify, however, that this has got nothing to do with racism. I have nothing against coloured birds. I have been called yellow myself many times. But I do hope the eatery changes its mascot to something slightly more appetizing. Despite my initial misgivings, their food turned out to be finger-licking delicious—perfectly grilled succulent chicken with an assortment of sauces, fries, vegetables and salads. I'm not surprised that they have claimed the position of being one of the most popular overseas restaurant chains in India. It's true about the queues too.

Success shouldn't go to their head though. It's time someone ruffled their feathers and did a revaluation. People may not have noticed the tiny black bird on the logo. But, having an oversized black one doing the bop outside the restaurants may be stretching it a little.

Time to say Bye Bye Birdie perhaps.

Bon appétit!

5.
To Smear or Not to Smear

Birthdays make me very nervous.

Perhaps I should be more specific. It's the birthday cake with layers of cream, chocolate and fruit that makes me uneasy. The gooey goodness that people usually take delight in eating or licking off their fingers. Except that they don't seem to want to do that anymore, in Gurgaon at least.

In a bizarre ritual, weirdly reminiscent of a pie fight, people start smearing birthday cake on one another as soon as the candles are blown out. It starts with a not-so-innocent dab of cream on the birthday person's cheek which soon turns into an overwhelming fiasco involving cake-smeared people, much running around and lots and lots of shrieking.

Remember the Instagram photograph of Indian cricket team captain M S Dhoni's icing-smeared face on his birthday recently? That is exactly what I am talking about.

I find the entire spectacle hugely disturbing, having grown up with the knowledge that birthday cakes were meant to be eaten, not vandalized. The fact that India is home to a quarter of the world's hungry people doesn't help the cause either.

As children we hung around expectantly near the dessert table, waiting for the cake to be cut so that we could get a delicious slice (or two) to consume all by ourselves. Having been a foodie even then, I would never have dreamed of wasting even a teeny-tiny morsel of that deliciousness. Also, the grown-ups those days would have made sure we were spanked soundly had we tried anything other than putting it in our mouths.

At my daughter's birthday parties, I find myself hovering menacingly near the centre table, glowering at anyone who dares extend their finger towards the icing. 'Cakes are meant to be eaten,' I warn the crowd gathered at my living room as soon as I find them exchanging naughty smiles at the start of the festivities. They dare not have other intentions.

I still remember the first birthday party when she was old enough to stand and cut the cake by herself. Dressed in a frothy pink party frock, she had just blown out the candles and was getting ready to cut a slice (with my help) when all hell broke loose. Dab, dab, dab, shrieks, screams, giggles were followed by loud wailing. It was all over in seconds and I had a bawling, cake-smeared shuddering mess in my hands. It took me days to clean my living room. Everywhere I looked, there was chocolate, cream and cake bits. The party frock (I had paid a bomb to buy) was ruined. It took a couple of birthdays with plain sponge cakes (sans cream) for the little girl and her mother to get over the trauma.

I wish I could blame it on the children. But they weren't the problem, really. Obviously, they got the idea from the adults who seem to think it's a tradition.

Like my neighbour Mrs Chopra for instance. Her birthday party the other day turned into an orgy of sorts. Except, instead of the sex, there was cake. Lots of it. Chocolate, cream and cherries! The woman was celebrating her 40th birthday party at a local pub. She had invited all her kitty party friends from the colony including me. My attempts to dissuade her from including me in the guest list for weeks hadn't worked.

'Don't be silly,' she had chided. 'How can I not invite you to my party? You're my BFF!' A sentiment I clearly did not reciprocate. Resigned to my fate, I arrived for the big bash. Her husband had ordered her a naughty cake. 'It's the custom, no? To have one,' she had giggled when she noticed the horrified expression of my face.

Once the pleasantries were over and the cocktails started flowing, the party got ugly. The cake was cut and the women started plastering Mrs Chopra and each other with cake and cream, a 'cake facial' as they called it. When I tried to protest, they shut me up with 'You must do it. It's a tradition.'

Seriously? Since when?

The only tradition that involves any kind of cake being vandalized during a festivity is a wedding tradition, which dates back to ancient Rome. Those days, it was considered good luck to break a dried cake or barley bread over the bride's head.

While most Indians (erroneously) believe that this cake-smearing madness came from the West, this is precisely the kind of thing that could get you killed if you lived abroad. A guy was stabbed a few years back in the United States because he smeared cake on his girlfriend's cheek during a party. Another woman in China got her friends to attack a guy who smeared her face with cake during a night out.

Now I don't blame these people at all. As you might have figured out, this kind of thing would get me quite agitated as well. So, if you are planning a birthday party sometime soon, now would be the time to strike me off your list.

It is high time we Villagers realized that birthday cakes are meant to be eaten, not smeared and destroyed. I hope Mrs Chopra is reading this.

At the tween's birthday party last year—the milestone birthday where she turned into a teenager—disaster struck once more. She was looking beautiful, all dressed up in a black cocktail dress paired with high heels (borrowed from me) to impress her friends. The cake was cut and it was like a cheap remake of *Final Destination* all over again. Trying to escape the gaggle of girls who wanted to smear cake on her (despite my repeated requests), she twisted her ankle and tore her ligament. Children these days do not listen to adults anymore.

Her father and me had to carry a howling teenager back to the car. The birthday was ruined. The poor thing was laid up in bed for almost a month in a cast, miserable that her milestone birthday had turned into such a horrific ordeal.

I guess it's just as well I don't carry a knife with me. I might be behind bars if I did.

6.
Adventures of the Road Runner

Every Sunday, I wake up to the sound of the loud Zumba music being played on loudpseakers somewhere in the distance. If this was any other day, I wouldn't have minded waking up at the crack of dawn to foot-tapping South American beats, but Sunday is my day of rest. My day to wake up late, spending what's left of the morning poring over newspapers and padding about the house in pyjamas for the rest of the day doing nothing much. Other than eating and sleeping that is.

Thanks to Raahgiri Day, restful Sundays are history now.

Let me tell you about Raahgiri first.

Raahgiri is a community initiative to reclaim the streets of Gurgaon every Sunday and make it non-accessible for motorized transport. Raahgiri had its origins in Colombia. The first *Ciclovia*, roughly translated as 'cycle way', was organized in Bogota in 1974 to oppose unsustainable urban development practices. This concept has been adopted by countries world-over, including our Village with Open Streets, Summer Streets, Happy Streets and Raahgiri Day being some of the names.

The entire Village gets together on Raahgiri Day, literally waking up at the crack of dawn, and spends the morning loitering about on the traffic-free roads doing Zumba, Pilates, Aerobics and an assortment of similar fitness activities. There are women sprawled on exercise mats demonstrating impossible yoga poses, children cycling around happily with their parents while senior citizens huddle together in groups, eating corn out of styrofoam cups and gossiping. There is bonhomie in the air. There are basketball matches, cricket matches and various other impromptu matches being played on the empty roads. As the morning wears on, Zumba music is replaced by Yo Yo Honey Singh blaring from the loudspeakers and music systems placed at regular intervals. The restaurants in the demarcated traffic-free zones are all open, serving hot, fresh food to the people moving from one activity to the other.

It's a brilliant idea, in principle. Except for people like me who hate waking up early on a Sunday and abhor anything to do with fitness or exercise. Not to mention Yo Yo Honey Singh.

Not just that. Last Sunday's Raahgiri Day got off to a rather bumpy start for me.

I almost got killed by a speeding car while trying to get to the thin strip of road cordoned off for pedestrians and cyclists in front of my condo. Not happy to be driving down half a road, car drivers are determined to make up for the lack of space with excessive speed on Raahgiri Sundays. I would have become a road crash statistic you'd read about in the news, much like the poor bloke on a cycle who got mowed down on his way to work a couple of days ago. Thankfully, someone up there had other plans for me and left me in one piece to finish the task I'm here to do in this world.

'You make such a mountain out of a molehill,' my friends told me later when I recounted my ordeal. 'Nothing would have happened. The car would have stopped.' The entire group gets together every Sunday to do yoga on the pavement and eat buckets of masala corn afterwards. 'You have to join us,' they had been pestering me for weeks. 'It's just yoga yaar, that can't harm you. It'll be fun. Please join us.'

I guess I am not destined to join them in their fitness endeavour. By the time I had navigated the roads and got to the group, yoga class was already over. The errant driver may have actually done me a favour!

I'm happy to report, however, that I did my bit to reclaim a part of Gurgaon's road. In fact, I even risked my life for it. The road, in question, a two-minute walk from my home, was full of people—cyclists, pedestrians, runners, children playing badminton, boys tossing footballs around, women and children exercising on bright blue mats, groups of people huddled together, gossiping, people-watching. Women and men in trendy active wear, kids and young adults on fancy bicycles, young and old, all of Gurgaon it seemed, huffing and puffing away as they navigated the stretch of the road available to them.

It was surreal and amidst it all, I kept having déjà vu moments that I couldn't quite shake off. There was a feeling that I had seen it all before. But where? Raahgiri Day was started in Gurgaon so I couldn't have witnessed it in any other city. And then it hit me. I remembered where I'd seen it before. A smile soon gave way to loud laughter, shocking a few of the people next to me, having their own private conversation. They rolled their eyes at me as I walked away, grinning from ear to ear, shaking my head.

Of course I'd seen it all before. Having lived most of my life in Kolkata, we had witnessed plenty of Raahgiri Days in a month. Days when we would be free to reclaim the streets from non-existent vehicular traffic, walking, running, cycling, playing cricket or football, sitting down under a shady nook to chit-chat with friends. Of course, at that time we didn't realize how big a service our politicians were doing us. Or how environmentally conscious they actually were.

Adventures of the Road Runner

If you haven't realized it already, back in those days Raahgiri Days were called Bandhs. And they happened ever so often that, in time, they lost most of their novelty. Walking or playing cricket on empty roads wasn't fun anymore. So many years down the line and miles away from home, I realize how good we had it then. And we didn't even know! The politicians we cribbed about were actually doing something good for the people.

I hear that the Raahgiri experiment has been so successful in Gurgaon that other areas in Delhi such as Connaught Place are planning to make car-free Sundays the norm. Raahgiri will now be adopted in forty Indian cities, they say. While I'm sure the cops will not be too happy about putting in extra hours on a Sunday to ensure that people can play hookey on the roads, the big picture looks bright. At least for the time being.

So I guess it's true then—the saying about what Bengal thinks today, India thinks tomorrow.

Raahgiri has certainly proved that. Perhaps I'll join the yoga class on Sunday after all.

7.
The Horrors of Halloween

It was eight in the evening and I was getting ready to settle down in front of the television when the bell rang. Several times. Loud and insistent.

Cursing under my breath, I ran to the front door and opened it.

Count Dracula stood outside, scowling at me. He was probably around eight, dark circles under his beady eyes and red lipstick smeared all over his mouth. He held a Meena Bazaar plastic bag under his arm which he thrust at me, somewhat rudely. 'Aunty, give me candy.' It wasn't a request, but an order.

'Aren't you forgetting something?' I asked him.

'Forgetting what?' Dracula Junior blinked at me. 'It's Halloween today. You are supposed to give me candy. Don't you know that?' I noticed that he was yelling but that didn't bother me. The last part of his statement made me wince, however. The underlying assumption that I was expected to fall in line with his demand.

Now I know he was merely a child but something about his attitude had started grating on my nerves.

'I know its Halloween and I will give you candy but aren't you forgetting something?' I asked him again.

He looked really angry now, eyes flashing. I could make out that he was used to getting his way at home. An image of an indulgent mother running to cater to every whim and fancy of the kid popped up in front of my eyes. I was sure the little fella would stamp his feet and have a hissy fit right in front of my door. Well, let him, I thought to myself, I do not like impudent children.

'Before you ask anyone for candy, you are supposed to say 'Trick or Treat' and wish them Happy Halloween. Don't you know that?' I told the little brat. It was really juvenile on my part but I'm sure you are not going to grudge me that. I couldn't help but smile when I delivered the last part of my sentence.

The vampire shrugged. The expression on his face said that he was bored and couldn't really care less. Could he have his candy now and leave?

I sighed and headed back to my kitchen. I didn't have a lot of sweets lying around but there was a packet of Cadbury's Eclairs left over from a birthday party. Grabbing a fistful of Eclairs, I walked back to where Dracula stood, fidgeting with his Meena Bazaar bag. 'Here you go,' I said, extending my arm to dump the sweets into his bag. He moved the bag away quickly staring at me as though I had morphed into a ghoul myself. 'Eclairs? *Kya aap ke paas achhe candies nahi hai?*' the scorn in his voice was unmistakeable.

I could have smacked him right then and there but I didn't. My fingers were itching desperately. 'What do you mean by achhe candies?' I asked innocently.

'Who on earth eats eclairs these days? Don't you have Ferraro Rocher or Sour Punk, Aunty?' Was that the hint of a smirk on the child's face?

I couldn't believe what I was hearing. 'No, I don't,' I said. 'This is all I have, you will just have to take these.'

'You could always give me money.' That brazen little...!

I regained my composure and told him coldly, 'I most certainly won't give you money. And now, if you'll excuse me, I have work to do. So please take these sweets or ring someone else's doorbell if you like!'

That monster. He stormed off in a huff, his red cape flying around him. I'm quite sure I heard him abuse under his breath.

I slammed the door shut.

Over the years, Halloween in Gurgaon has become a frightening experience for me and it has nothing to do with witches and warlocks. I'm scared of the ill-mannered little children (read: brats) who land up at my door demanding outrageous things. Foreign candy, money, the list goes on.

Gurgaon's Halloween phenomenon is fairly recent though, the expat population having imported the spook fest to the city. What's alarming is the gigantic proportions the festival has assumed in the last ten years or so. Everyone in the Millennium City celebrates Halloween these days. Kids dress up and go from door to door collecting candy.

It's not just the children. The adults dress up and throw Halloween parties. You will find party shops all over Gurgaon stocking imported Halloween costumes and accessories to be bought at astronomical prices for these parties. I've been invited to a few myself but I've had to decline politely. Spending the evening dressed as Morticia Adams sipping a Bloody Mary is not exactly my idea of fun. The funny thing is, I'm quite sure if you quizzed these Halloween enthusiasts about the origins of the festival, they wouldn't have a clue. Like most things in Gurgaon, this one is a fad too.

Growing up, the only exposure I had to Halloween was through comic books, storybooks, movies and the occasional postcard sent by a relative abroad with a picture of some kid dressed up as a ghoul holding a giant jack-o'-lantern.

My daughter was invited to a birthday party on Halloween

once. When all the guests had assembled at the birthday girl's house, the mother had sent all the kids out to collect candy from the neighbours. The chocolates, sweets and chips that the kids got as loot was the food served at the party. If you can call that serving food. I was horrified when I heard the story, making a mental note never to send the girl for Halloween-themed birthday parties again.

I don't think it's a terribly good idea to send your kids to a stranger's house asking for candy. It is asking for trouble, in my opinion. Renting out exorbitant costumes to dress children is also a no-no in my books. If you really must dress them, why not put some thought and let the kids create the costumes themselves? Still, I'd be willing to tolerate it all if the children, in question, were better-behaved and minded their Ps and Qs. I am not very good with entitled brats.

I had lousier luck for the rest of the evening. An assortment of ghosts, ghouls, vampires and witches came calling, asking for expensive candy and money. Some had maids in tow, lurking about furtively while the kids made the demands. These were all sorts of scary creatures, dressed in the finest of clothes. I could hear them laughing in the corridors outside. 'I will drink your blood,' one of them was threatening the other, rather dramatically in Hindi. 'I'm a vampire, I will bite your flesh!' Loud shrieks, squeals and howls echoed in the stairwell throughout the evening.

I've never been more frightened my whole life. What horrors are we unleashing onto the world, I wonder.

8.
Ek Bottle Vodka

The little boy at the grocery shop was bored. I couldn't really blame him. Grocery stores bore the hell out of me too He wouldn't have been more than eight years old. I watched him, out of the corner of my eye, as he tried, unsuccessfully, to clamber onto one of the shopping trolleys lying idle on one side of the aisle. The trolley skidded, hitting the wall with a loud clang. He jumped off quickly and looked at his parents furtively. They weren't looking at him. They were busy inspecting labels on pickle jars in another section of the store.

After desperately trying to get his parents' attention for several minutes by trying some death defying stunts, he yelled out to them, loudly, '*Pappa, chalo na daaru kharidte hain!*' Pappa, a harassed-looking, pot-bellied man instantly turned purple while the mother, bejewelled and saree-clad with vermillion on her forehead, ran across to where the little boy was standing, grabbed him roughly by the shoulders and instantly steered him towards the entrance of the shop with a 'shhhhhhhh!'

Everyone at the store, including me, was amused. I didn't understand why the parents were mortified. Clearly, the father drank alcohol in front of the child and liquor shopping was a favourite father-son outing. But why do it in front of the child if you are ashamed to own up to it later?

I could, however, completely relate to why the little boy thought a liquor store was a more fun place to hang out in than a grocery store. As an adult, I find Gurgaon's liquor vends quite fascinating, unlike anything I've ever seen before. Makeshift shacks scattered all across the Village where people merrily consume alcohol, out in the open, under the twinkling night sky. There are tiny stalls set up next to the shacks, which sell an assortment of snacks to go with the beverages. Tandoori chicken, kababs and various other fried food. The aroma assails your nostrils if you happen to drive by.

I remember being scandalized by this culture of open-air drinking when I had arrived in Gurgaon, some twenty years back. We were on our way to buy groceries one evening when I noticed a couple of young men, standing by the side of their blue Maruti van, beer and other alcohol bottles neatly lining the roof of the car.

'What on earth are these fellows up to?' I asked in surprise.

Born and bred in a city such as Kolkata, where people drank inside their homes or in clubs and restaurants, I was slightly shocked to see people flaunting their alcohol publicly in full view of everyone. Even the liquor bottles that were bought in Kolkata were neatly wrapped in newspaper so that no one could make out what the packages contained. No prizes for guessing what the package contained but no one really flaunted liquor openly.

'They are drinking beer, what else?' my husband said casually. 'And probably some whisky and vodka as well,' he squinted his eyes to make out the labels on the bottles.

'Here?' I said. 'Right in the middle of nowhere?' I was horrified.

'Oh, it's not in the middle of nowhere. Look behind you, there's a liquor shack.'

He was right. I looked around to where he was pointing to see a tiny shack, dimly lit with a clumsy signboard that said

'IMFL liquor sold here.' A young boy was stringing some pieces of chicken into a skewer getting them ready for a charcoal pit nearby.

'What's IMFL?' I remember asking.

'Indian Made Foreign Liquor,' said my husband.

The liquor vends with their kabab counters still exist, twenty years later. In principle though. They've become bigger stores with fancy signboards that scream 'English Wine Store' or 'European Wines' and the makeshift kabab counters have morphed into air-conditioned drinking rooms which serve loud music and an assortment of dubious world cuisine ranging from Tibetan to Chinese and Indian. The drinking rooms are full of noisy youngsters, looking for a place to unwind after a busy day at work in their MNC offices or call centres. Well, at least they don't have liquor bottles stacked on the roof of their cars anymore.

There are bigger stores in the swanky malls which sell IMFL and foreign booze and for a small price you can get your bottles home delivered.

While there is a lot of debate about how Gurgaon's liquor shacks have contributed to a law and order problem in the Millennium City, the jury is still out on that one. The Village continues to be a favourite watering hole for folks from Delhi and other parts of Haryana.

I can't help but wonder whether the father obliged the son and took him daru shopping that evening. I have a sneaky suspicion that instead of the tandoori chicken treat the little boy was expecting while his father stocked up on his weekly stash, he got a sound wallop instead.

Poor chap.

9.

Party Pooper

Parties are quite the rage in the Millennium City. Booze is cheap and free-flowing, there are plenty of pubs, restobars, lounges and farmhouses in the vicinity and denizens love letting their hair down and having a good time. It's not just the people, animals party here too. Canine birthday parties are the rage here. I'll tell you about that another day!

My neighbours, the Chopras, have been throwing gala parties regularly to get over the grief at having to give their dog Lucky up for adoption. Lucky, a Saint Bernard, had grown too big to be kept in the flat. Since Mr Chopra works in a Japanese firm, all their parties are Japanese themed. Let's just say that if I see another plate of tandoori sushi, I will scream.

Gone are the days when an invitation to a party filled the heart with much joy. But then, life is so different when you are six and have an evening of birthday cake, games and take-home goodies to look forward to. Sigh! At the wrong side of 40, I find my heart sinking at the thought of another party in Gurgaon. Joy has been replaced by dread and the only *piñata* I look forward to smashing has an uncanny resemblance to the host's head!

If all of this sounds rather extreme to you, perhaps you haven't had the good fortune to be invited to the wrong kind of parties.

Thank your lucky stars. If you had, you might have seen the woman sulking in the corner, glowering at all and sundry, blaming the world for her misfortune. Yes, I'm the one who couldn't get away.

Do you feel my pain? Read on to find out whether you have been to any of these Gurgaon do's:

Musical soiree
This one is strangely reminiscent of a hostage crisis. You and a motley group of individuals are taken captive by the host or hostess and tortured by an unending medley of songs (original or covers)/instrument recitals/recitation/impromptu dance performances. One after another. If that wasn't enough, there are a few people recording your agony on their smartphones, though I don't think any television channel would be interested in airing this show. There's no way you can escape. The doors are locked. You might consider jumping out of the balcony in extreme cases. Death seems preferable to this ordeal.

Potluck party
This one makes *Breaking Bad* look like Candy Land. This isn't the kind of potluck party where you show up with Tupperware filled with your signature curry. Potluck means *pot*-luck. Everyone around you is puffing away to glory, squinting their eyes and laughing a great deal. They are on top of the world while you stumble from one corner to the next trying to find some clean air to breathe. Gasp!

Selfie party
You better have your best clothes on for this one. Picture perfect make-up and not a hair out of place. Oh, did I forget the pout? The hostess will corner you at every step, whip out her smartphone and click selfies. One near the stairs, another next to the dining

table, another one on the balcony. Oh dear, the light is too dim on the balcony, my double chin looks exaggerated. Let's get one with the dog and the goldfish in the bowl instead. If you are lucky, you can throw her smartphone out the window when she's not looking. Dogs don't just eat homework these days. That's your excuse.

Spiritual party
This one is a real nuisance if you are a non-believer like me. You can't hurt the host's feeling or religious sentiments so you fall in line without overt protest. If you think the ordeal ends with the prayers, you're wrong. There's song and dance too. Much swaying, clapping and waving of hands. Perhaps you can stretch your arms out a wee bit and strangle the host. That might end the agony.

Housewarming party
This one should be called 'Buy Me a Present Party' because that is what you are expected to do. Buy a ridiculously expensive gift in exchange for a conducted tour around someone's new home. Marvel at the godawful décor, bizarre colour scheme and the rather strange curios and paintings the host brought back from his or her latest trip (read: Chatuchak Market) abroad. I'd rather courier the gift and skip the tour.

Office party
You see them every single day of the year. Why on earth would you want to socialize with them over some flat Coca-Cola, chips and stale pizza while Daler Mehndi belts out ancient *balle balle* numbers over a music system? Oh wait, there's Antakshari too. You are herded into a circle and you have to start singing Bollywood songs. A for *Aaja Aaja Mein Hoon Pyar Tera!* Arrrrrrgh, come and kill me now!

Kiddie birthday party

Three words for this one. Are you nuts? Wailing children, maids in tow and yummy mummies do not make a good party. There's one person in the crowd who looks sorrier than you do—the magician that the host hired to do magic tricks for the little brats. Wait a minute, isn't he getting paid for the magic tricks? If you pay me, I might show you a trick. I will do the disappearing act for you!

Wellness party

If you think discussing nutrition, dietary supplements and fitness was my idea of fun, you might want to take a hike. Literally and figuratively. It would do you a world of good. Keep me far away from the nuts and seeds. Those are for birds and I'm not one. In fact, I don't particularly like birds or bird food. The lecture on transfats will be wasted on me so spare me the invite. I'm going to Wendy's instead. I have a date with their Baconator!

Diwali party

I'm quite sure Agatha Christie was invited to a Diwali party once and her angst at the ordeal drove her to write *Cards on the Table* where the host Mr Shaitana was murdered after a bridge get-together! Get the drift? I'm a writer too and I might end up murdering you in my next book. So, save me the invite and keep your cards close to your chest for this one!

Theme party

Dressing up as Morticia Addams for an entire evening is not my thing. Don't get me wrong. I love ghosts and ghouls but only in books and movies. I don't want to mingle with them in a party over chicken tikka kabab and breezers. I'm not too fond of movie stars either so don't expect me to turn up with my bouffant hairstyle, flared pants and oversized goggles if you are planning a Bollywood retro party. I tried to make myself look like Whitney Houston for a party once when I was a teen but an allergic reaction to the lacquer from the perm made my face swell up like a puffer fish. Need I say more?

10.

Gurgaon Ink

'Oh my god! Did you get yourself a tattoo, finally?' my friend Sonali suddenly shrieked out in excitement. We were having lunch at the new Chinese restaurant that had opened in a nearby mall. I had reached out for the bowl of hakka noodles and she had spotted the rose on my wrist, peeping out from under the sleeve of the sweater. The other diners at the restaurant stared at us curiously, probably wondering what the shriek was all about.

Suddenly self-conscious, I pulled the sweater sleeve down, hiding the portion of the wrist previously on display. 'It's not a tattoo,' I mumbled, avoiding her stare, cheeks flushed.

'What do you mean it's not a tattoo, what is it then?' Sonali looked confused.

I didn't know what to say. The truth is, I had been playing with my daughter last evening and she had pulled out an enormous collection of stick-on tattoos (for children) from her cupboard—from Disney princesses to superheroes and science fiction.

'Where on earth did you get these?' I had asked her, amazed.

'I collected them over the years from various birthday parties,' she had replied, busy sorting out the sheets. 'Wanna try some?'

I had nodded and we had spent the rest of the evening, giggling, splashing each other with water and trying on tattoos.

The rose had come out of a Disney Princesses sheet. I think it was the rose from *Beauty and the Beast*.

I didn't realize that it would be a conversation-stopper at lunch. With tattoos being the latest style statement in the Millennium City, I did not want to come off as fashion-challenged by saying it was a child's stick on tattoo. Who on earth would want to commit social *harakiri* (Japanese ritual suicide) like that? Instead, I cleverly changed the conversation.

'Can we order some fried rice? I don't like these noodles at all, they're too spicy!'

Growing up, the only person I knew who had a tattoo was Popeye. And he wasn't even real. A comic book sailor, with a voice that would put Himesh Reshammiya to shame, he had a gigantic anchor tattooed on his arm and ate spinach. Hardly a role model for a little girl. Some of our house help, who came from neighbouring villages and the Sunderbans area, also had tattoos on their arms and wrists. Gods and Goddesses, initials and sundry other objects from their daily lives.

On my travels abroad, I noticed the heavily tattooed members of the Hells Angels Motorcycle Club and added bikers to my list (of people with tattoos). BBC and the Hairy Bikers validated that entry. So, before I arrived in Gurgaon, my list had three entries: comic book characters, villagers and bikers.

Imagine my surprise when I found out that having a tattoo in Gurgaon puts you in the list of who's who and you-know-whos! Not just that, I've also witnessed a mind-boggling selection of tattoos here. Dragons, flora and fauna, hearts, angels, letters of the alphabet… you name it and I'm sure to have seen it! Every second person I bump into seems to have gotten themselves inked. Not once, but often twice or thrice. A dear friend is contemplating her fourth one. Yes, the one that shrieked. She came to my house last week with a drawing. It was an elaborate Tree of Life that she wanted tattooed at the nape of her neck. Ouch.

Most of my friends have gotten 'engraved' over the last year and I'm under tremendous pressure to get one myself. There is a slight problem though. Having been jabbed several times over the course of my life by well-meaning doctors, I have developed a fright from needles. In fact, I started this year with the resolution that I would never go near a needle if I could help it. But how was I to know that tattoos would make it so hard to stick to the straight and narrow? And while I don't want to end up looking like Popeye before the year is out, I do want to fit in with the Janes and the rest of Gurgaon's hip and happening.

'*Aap ek tattoo karwa lijiye*,' my neighbour Mrs Chopra told me recently. She is not hip or happening and struggles to string together two words in English. But, she's got her sights set on the right places. She loves to shop at 'Jaara' and recently bought herself some flashy designer accessories. She even convinced her husband to shell out an obscene amount of money and got herself inked on her wrist. The new job has made him generous, it seems. 'My haasbund's initials,' she offered coyly when she saw me staring. 'He's very heppy and it looks nice, no?'

I don't know what to say.

'If you don't want a tattoo on your body, you can always get one on your teeth,' she adds.

'What the...?' I can't believe what I'm hearing.

'Yes,' she says. 'I'm going to get a picture of Lucky on my tooth.' Lucky was her Saint Bernard who she had to give up for adoption. The poor woman has not been able to get over the grief of losing him.

It seems that tooth tattoos are painless. One can get a cap with the tattoo placed on the tooth. You can also remove it when you get bored of it.

It's really getting to me now. All parts of my body actually.

Gurgaon Ink 209

I've even started following episodes of LA Ink religiously on the telly, and Hairy Biker when I'm feeling hungry. All those biker dudes and chicks with the amazing body art. But I can't seem to overcome my fear of injections and infections.

What to do, that's just me and all my phobias. Instead I find myself, rummaging through my daughter's cupboards for her temporary tattoos. She's used up all of them, that brat. I think I helped! All that's left is Sleeping Beauty and Stich. Wondering which of these would be age appropriate.

Any guesses?

11.

Unfaithfully Yours

Of late, Gurgaon's favourite topic seems to be infidelity. At coffee meets, book clubs, lunch parties—after a bit of polite conversation, an awkward pause and then, the inevitable. The latest scoop on who's doing who, and who doesn't know. There's just no escaping it.

Just the other day, I was hungrily tucking into a dim sum lunch at a popular Chinese eatery when a couple I knew very well walked in. Desperately trying not to choke on my *sui mai*, I downed copious quantities of Coca-Cola in a hurry. You see, the reason for my discomfort was that 'the couple', in question, were not married to each other and I knew both their spouses extremely well. They even had two teenagers between them.

Now, don't get me wrong, I'm no prude but I wished, at that very moment, that I was dining elsewhere.

'The couple,' however, did not seem to be bothered. Politely nodding their heads at me, the two seated themselves in a quiet corner, as far as possible from the rest of the diners. I marvelled at their quiet confidence, arrogance almost. Not worried that they would be spotted or that word would get back to their homes.

'Is infidelity on the rise in Gurgaon?' my friend whispered across the table. 'People are so open about these things these days.' I shrugged. I really didn't know whether more and more people were allowing themselves to be carried away by reckless adventures of the body and soul in the Millenium City throwing caution to the winds. What I did know, for a fact, was that it was certainly easier to do so. Have a reckless adventure that is.

When I moved to Gurgaon, nineteen years ago, there weren't any places to get adventurous or reckless in. Just vast, empty spaces and a few buildings scattered in between. No fancy malls, restaurants, lounges or pubs. Not even a darkened multiplex to hold hands in. Hardly any place to have an intimate date. Just your own home or outside, in the lap of nature.

Cutting to the present, there are a bewildering variety of places to choose from—hotels, motels, heritage havelis, guest houses, lodges. Gurgaon's construction boom has reaped rich dividends for unlikely recipients! One is literally spoilt for choice if one wants to canoodle with a lover. Legally or illegally. There are also coffee shops, book shops and the neighbourhood swimming pool!

Surprised? I was too. The swimming pool would never have struck me as a place to have a romantic rendezvous in but events in the recent past changed my mind. Our pool is noisy and crowded at all times with bathers from the vicinity. Uncles, aunties, grandmas, teenage boys and girls. During hot summer evenings, it's like the Ganges during Kumbh Mela.

Mrs Malhotra, the one I discovered at the coffee shop with the swimming instructor, is a regular at our pool. She's tall and shapely, curves in all the right places, a regular yummy Gurgaon mummy. Both our daughters used to take swimming lessons last year. While they can manage well on their own now, swimming expertly up and down the length of the pool without help, it's the mother who needs the coach now. Not for swimming lessons though.

I've been seeing her almost every day at the club. With the summer vacations on, the little girl and myself have been going swimming every single day to beat the dreadful heat. The rectangular pool is surrounded on all sides by tall, leafy trees. There are cane chairs and tables placed by the side of the pool where people can sit and have a drink before or after a swim.

On most days, I find Mrs Malhotra perched by the side of the pool in her dark brown tankini, bosom spilling out, making eyes at Sushant, the coach. Sushant is a stocky, swarthy-complexioned chap who gives lessons to the members' kids for a fee. He's not good-looking in the traditional sense of the term but he has twinkling eyes and a pleasant smile. I've seen many of the other women give him the once-over.

I hear that it's quite common in Gurgaon to have a fling with the gym instructor or even the yoga teacher. Something to do with endorphins and affairs. Our swimming instructor is not immune to Mrs Malhotra's charms either. He doesn't have eyes for anyone else but her. The kids splashing about in the pool under his care may as well have been invisible for all the attention he gives them. She giggles, dipping her feet in the pool suggestively and he swims over to where she is. They giggle, lean towards each other, giggle some more. PDA is in full view.

I'm at the far end of the pool, submerged in the water, watching the entire spectacle keenly. Everyone in and around the pool is watching as well. There's pin-drop silence, none of the noisy chatter one hears every evening. What a brave woman, I think to myself. Not bothered about people watching her in action or being spotted by someone she knows. Running into someone familiar was quite likely in a place as small as this. The woman doesn't look as though she could be bothered. Unperturbed even as Sushant swims circles around her dangling feet. She doesn't get into the pool the whole time as I am there. She merely sits by the edge and dips her feet in from time to time.

Did she even know how to swim?

Unfaithfully Yours 213

I found out the answer to that soon enough.

You see, while everyone is busy watching the poolside tableau, Mrs Malhotra's husband walks up the path to the pool to have a quick swim straight after work. I've seen Mr Malhotra in our complex. He's an average-looking man, short with thinning hair. I don't know either of them very well. They are good friends with my neighbour Mrs Chopra. She tells me that they had an arranged marriage. 'No love shuv, their parents fixed the match. Do you think she would have fallen in love with him?'

As soon as Mrs Malhotra spots her husband, she freezes, eyes peeled to a spot right behind where I'm resting after a few laps. I turn my head back to see Mr Malhotra walking busily towards the changing room. He hasn't noticed his wife on the other end. Sushant too seems transfixed, not sure what to do.

And then it happened.

Mrs Malhotra drops into the pool rather clumsily with a loud splash. I guess the intention was to avoid being seen. It might have worked otherwise as the husband did not notice her. But the noisy splash makes him turn his head abruptly to see where it came from.

The wife doesn't know how to swim. She has never swum a day in her life. The show by the poolside with her tankini was for Sushant's benefit. As soon as she is in the water, she starts choking, desperately throwing her hands about, trying to rise to the surface. '*Bachao! Mujhe Bachao!* I can't swim... glub glub... I can't swim,' she starts shrieking, her head bobbing in and out of the miniscule waves she had stirred up with her hands.

Mr Malhotra rushes over to the spot as soon as he hears the familiar voice.

'Jaanu? What on earth are you doing in the pool? You don't know how to swim!'

What happened next was not a pleasant sight. The woman

had to be fished out of the water by Sushant, Mr Malhotra and some other bathers. I had kept a safe distance all throughout. Mr Malhotra had fetched a towel, wrapped his shivering wife with it and sent her to the changing room to get dressed. I saw them leaving together ten minutes later. Him walking briskly up ahead, her following behind, head bowed. I couldn't see Sushant. Perhaps he had run off to hide.

Mrs Chopra tells me the couple are getting divorced. 'Arre, there was a big scandal with her, don't you know? She was having an affair with the swimming instructor! Can you imagine the disgrace? He found out about it! Very sad, no?' Mrs Chopra had no idea I was there. I'm not likely to tell her either.

It is very sad. My sympathies are for the husband though. The woman was clearly out of her depth. He may have left her high and dry but at least she's not swimming with the fishes!

12.

Gurugram Gymming

It wasn't always this way, you know. This aversion to exercise and all things fitness-related.

Many years ago, when I first moved to the Millennium City, I too harboured a secret desire of being lean and mean like an average Gurgaon aunty. A sexy, well-toned body was something to aspire to. But a visit to a local gym dashed my hopes to the ground. Not just that, the experience left me scarred for life. I vowed never to set foot inside a gym again.

You probably shouldn't either, if you are anything like me, with a low tolerance for uncouth people. Gurgaon has a whole lot of them and you are likely to run into them at the gym. A friend of mine has a personal trainer to help her work out at home. While that is prohibitively expensive, she doesn't mind the expense as it keeps the annoying people out of her way.

If you are headed to a gym in the Village any time soon, here's a list of people to watch out for:

The Machine Hoggers
These are the people who will go on using the machines at the gym for hours on end. They don't care about the lengthening queues of people waiting for a turn. No, these people do not

believe in sharing. It's almost as though the gym has been created only for their use. A polite 'excuse me? Are you finishing up at the treadmill?' will be greeted by a blank stare and then… nothing. They will go on walking on the damn thing as though you never existed. Or perhaps smile and tell you 'Oh hey, I just started using this. You will have to wait.' Yeah, as though I don't have a watch. I know you've been on it for hours! Even the gym instructors and the polite lady who sits behind the desk at the entrance is powerless. After waiting for a couple of hours, maybe even more, you leave the gym in a huff, never to return.

The Sweat Leavers
We all know that exercise releases happy chemicals called endorphins. Did you know that exercise also releases sweat? Lots and lots of smelly, icky sweat. So you always need to carry a towel to mop up if you are the kind who sweats like a pig. The sweat leavers don't seem to know that. There are the people who leave a trail of sweat, wherever they have been, Eww! On the handles of the exercise bike, the multi-gym, even the plastic ball they've been using to work on their pelvic region. You can find your way back to them if you follow the trail. And give them the dressing down they are not likely to forget. Not that it is likely to make much of a difference. You will find them without a towel again the next day!

The Smellies
These people have not discovered the deodorant or are under the impression that they don't need any. Unfortunately for you, you can smell them from a distance. With these people around, the gym smells as though something died in there. Then, there is the second kind of smelly who doesn't bathe yet sprays herself or himself with perfume or aftershave. Okay, now the gym smells like an animal died in an exotic flower garden. Perhaps this would

be a good time to tell them about the shower cubicle in the gym? Or run for the exit!

The Flirty Aunties

There is a reason gyms have instructors. An assortment of young lads who are meant to help you devise a workable exercise routine, help negotiate the machines and generally keep an eye on you as you work up a sweat. 'Open your laags Madamji', 'Spraad your thaigheej' are not invitations to have sex with them. They are simply doing their job, albeit in very poor English. But what to do? They are like that only. You need to remember that they are definitely not around for aimless chatting, sharing juicy bits of gossip, batting your eyelids at, or flirting. Now, the flirty aunties at the gym don't seem to know that. You will find them perpetually hovering around the instructors and monopolizing them at every corner. 'Mujhe help kar dijiye na please', is a refrain you will hear quite often and wince. You wonder how they get any serious exercise done. Perhaps the action on the side more than makes up for it.

The Obnoxious Music Lovers

Last and certainly not the least, if the gym is playing the most atrocious music, these are the people to blame. They make Bappi Lahiri sound like Hanz Zimmer. *Tutak Tutak Tutiya* is their favourite exercise number and they will threaten the management (perhaps by waving a gun) to make sure the song is playing every hour of the day till you have the song coming out of every aperture in your body. Then, there is a toxic cocktail of Yo Yo Honey Singh, Badshah and Hard Kaur interspersed in between. You can forget about Sia, Weeknd and David Guetta unless you are ready to bribe the manager to play your favourite music. Don't bother as that won't work. These are the big guns we are talking about. Literally. The easiest thing to do would be to leave. So you do just that.

13.

Every Dog Has Its Day

I've been invited to a birthday party. Much as I loathe children's birthday parties, I just couldn't get out of this one. The girl has just turned one and her parents (who happen to be close friends) blackmailed me into accepting with the line 'but she will be so disappointed if you don't land up. She absolutely adores you!'

That was true. The little girl did love me. Almost as much as her own parents. She would be all over me each time I visited, showering wet sloppy kisses on my face, finally settling near my feet with her toys while I chatted with her parents. Not without reason, of course. I have spent many mornings minding her while her mother was out running errands or visiting an elderly relative. We would spend those mornings going on quiet walks in our condo. I would allow her to run around in our park and buy her treats from the shops nearby.

It wouldn't be all that bad, I told myself as I got ready for the big day. She was such a lovable kid. I'm sure her friends would be the same. With that thought in mind, I arrived at a park in the neighbourhood nearby, the venue for the party, with a neatly wrapped gift.

A section of the park, which also had a tiny splash pool, had been decorated with colourful streamers and balloons. These had been strung up artfully from the trees that lined the outer fringes of the park. The wooden benches were covered with printed tablecloths and there were chairs for the guests to sit on. I could see that the guests had arrived—the birthday girl's friends from the building, accompanied by their parents. The mother was handing out party hats for the children to wear. Music was playing. Baha Men were singing *Who let the dogs out. Who? Who? Who?*

'You're late!' the mother had spotted me and rushed towards me, looking cross. 'You were supposed to come an hour earlier to help with the setting up. Vikram is over there getting the games organized,' she pointed to a spot at the far end of the park near the trees where the father and two young chaps were hunched over a wooden cardboard box.

'I'm sorry but looks like you have everything under control,' I laughed. Frisky, the birthday girl, had come bounding across to me. We hugged each other for a while before she ran off towards the wooden benches, nose twitching in excitement. A couple of young domestic helpers had started bringing out the refreshments. I could see that there were bowls of milk, flavoured chews, an assortment of cupcakes and a two-tiered birthday cake.

No sooner had the food been placed on the table, all hell broke loose. Or should I say the dogs. Yes, I'm talking about the dogs. Whose birthday party did you think it was? Frisky is a dog, an adorable Labrador belonging to my friends!

Anyway, back to the story. I think it was Badshah the Alsatian who started the trouble. He was a handsome fellow, tall and regal, black and brown fur all over. He was keeping his distance from the ladies, keeping his eyes trained on them all the while. His mummy, Mrs Chatterjee, a voluptuous woman in her early thirties was keeping a hand on his leash while she prattled with the other mummies at the party.

As soon as Reena, one of the young helpers, had placed the

last of the food on the wooden benches, Badshah made a sudden lunge for the birthday cake. His mummy, talking excitedly about the saree sale at Meena Bazaar, was taken aback, the leash pulled roughly from her grasp. She was thrown off the chair, landing on the grass with a loud *thwack*. She looked around, disoriented, yelling 'Badshah! Bad Dog!' But Badshah was already on the bench, sniffing the cake. The next instant, the other dogs, Fluffy, Rover, Tiny, Whiskers, Shiny and Goldie had broken free from their leashes and were clambering onto the table as well.

Frisky, standing obediently, by the side of her mother, watched all of this in horror, tail wagging in despair. Or was it excitement. She had never seen anything like it. 'Vikram, do something yaar,' the mother yelled to the dad. He stood frozen by the side of the cardboard box containing the party games. It didn't look as though they'd be of much use now.

'Frisky, stay!' my friend warned her daughter, who was now tugging on her leash, desperate, to join the action. The dishevelled mummies were crowding around the table trying to get their children down and salvage the food. The dogs were growling. Fur was about to fly.

I can't say I blame Badshah. A cake made out of meat and eggs. The smell was too tantalizing for him to ignore. He couldn't be expected to mind his manners. He was a dog after all. He had to have a slice. Maybe even the whole thing. What did he know about sharing?

The rest of the party was a disaster. Once the brawling dogs had been separated, their mummies had to march them home, tightly holding on to their leashes and their tempers. The food was destroyed, well not quite, the dogs had eaten up most of it. Party games remained in the cardboard box. Not that the dogs cared. They had much more fun taking bites of each other (and the food) on top of the table. As far as parties go, this

Every Dog Has Its Day

was their wildest.

My friends stood by the entrance to the park, handing out the take home gifts, special monogrammed leashes, to the guests when they left. Everyone looked shamefaced. Frisky was sitting next to them, party hat on her head, looking slightly confused. She nuzzled my hand when I reached out to pat her on the head.

'What a disaster this was yaar,' Vikram was scratching his head, staring hard at the ground. He looked despondent. 'I mean how could this have happened? Dog birthday parties are all the rage in the Gurgaon. I've been to a few myself. I've never seen this happening. What ill-mannered children!' His wife nodded in agreement, squeezing his hand in solidarity.

'Never mind, let's go clean up,' she said. 'If we leave the park like this, the Residents Association will make us pay a fine.'

All three of us and the young domestic helpers trudged off to clean the mess. It took us a while, scraping off remnants of cake, bits of chew and soggy napkins from the wooden table, sweeping the grass beneath. Frisky sat quietly in the corner, chewing on something she found lying around. The music was still playing. No one had turned it off.

Get back ruffy, Get that scruffy
Get back you flea infested mongrel

14.

Between a Rock and a Hard Place

Mrs Chopra has a broken heart. It's love that did it.

Now before you start thinking this is another tale about star-crossed lovers in the Millennium City, let me tell you that it's nothing of the sort. Mr Chopra didn't catch his wife canoodling in the swimming pool with her bae. Mrs Chopra has no plans of canoodling with her bae or anyone else. She's not that type at all. For her, a bae is someone who cleans peoples' homes in Mumbai. She's besotted with her pati, in sickness or in health, through thick or thin. She has no idea that 'thin' would cause her such distress though.

You see, like most Gurgaon ladies, she expects to be pampered by her husband with wine, chocolates, flowers, dinner and expensive gifts on Valentine's Day each year. This year too, the poor woman has been excited about it for several months. She's even called me a couple of times, unable to contain her excitement. 'Did you know? Valentine's Day is in two months' time. I'm so excited. I hope Chopra Sahab gets me something nice,' she says.

'Do you have something in mind?' I ask her. I'm quite sure there's something she's set her mind on acquiring. Last year, it was a Swarovski set. 'I do, I do,' she giggles coyly. 'I've seen this stunning diamond ring at the jewellery shop. It's half a carat on a claw setting. I've even dropped a few hints to him about how much that ring would suit me. I hope he gets it!'

'What are you getting him?' I ask her. There's silence on the other end of the line.

'I never get him anything. It's the woman who gets the gifts no? Not the men.' she says.

I'm quite amused by her behaviour. I've noticed plenty of my friends behaving in a similar fashion around this time, desperately hoping their husbands, lovers or significant others would shower lavish gifts on them as an expression of their undying commitment and love. Wine, chocolates, stuffed toys, clothes, jewellery, food—the list goes on. The thought of getting something for their partners in return never crosses their mind.

Valentine's Day is Gurgaon's love fest. Like Halloween, the celebration of love in the Millennium City often assumes alarming proportions. From the early morning newspapers plastered with offers and freebies to salons, stores and restaurants, everyone has a deal for couples on this day.

Malls are thronging with men buying last-minute gifts for their beaus, beauty salons crammed with women getting a quick touch-up job, restaurants are overbooked and overpriced with exotic, romantic menus on offer and one has to wait for hours to get a bite to eat. There are impatient crowds everywhere making last-minute dashes for…things! Wine shops are out of wine, supermarkets out of chocolate. I almost got knocked down by some rowdy teenagers outside a shop specializing in greeting cards and knick-knacks at the neighbourhood market. They were on a gift-buying mission for their girlfriends, what else?

The scales, of course, are heavily tipped in the favour of women on the day. I wonder what's in store for Mrs Chopra. The husband is a generous man. Over the years, I've seen him go to great lengths to get his biwi something good. Jewellery, overseas vacations, designer clothes. He even threw her a surprise birthday party when she turned forty!

When I call her up in the evening to find out, she's in tears.

'What's wrong,' I ask, concerned.

'Arre,' she sobs. 'You know how much I wanted the diamond ring. I was hoping he would get it for me.'

'And?' I ask.

'Do you know what he got me finally? I can't believe he would do something like this,' she says angrily, in between sobs.

'What did he get you?' I ask, exasperated. What could he have done that had reduced her to tears like this?

After a few minutes of coaxing, when she finally tells me, I can't stop giggling hysterically.

'Why are you laughing? It's not funny at all,' she says angrily and banged the phone down in a huff.

I collapsed on the sofa in giggles.

After having his fancy car stolen recently, Mr Chopra has decided to go on an austerity drive. Only his wife doesn't know that. With the recent demonetization and the ATMs running dry, he's decided to keep his declaration of love simple. Since he was a little short of cash in his wallet and didn't have a car to drive around with, he walked down to the post office next door and bought his wife a page of scented stamps in fragrances of rose, coffee and vanilla.

'I read in the papers that the post office had bought out these stamps for Valentine's Day. Isn't it a super idea? Remember the days when we used to write letters to each other, Jaanu? These stamps reminded me of that. They are scented also!' the man had rambled on, not noticing the ashen look on the wife's face.

A rose-scented stamp?

She's not talking to him for days now. She's not talking to me either.

Silly Mr Chopra. He should have known that diamonds, not stamps, are a girl's best friend!

Made in the USA
Monee, IL
03 May 2026

49438770R00134